BE A BUSINESS
ROCKSTAR

Teach Your Talents | Share Your Skills | Live Your Passion

Emma Holmes

Dedication

My wonderful hero of a husband, Jonathan, for his unvarying support EVEN when he thinks that I'm REALLY wrong & my beautiful little people Jack & Maggie.

Acknowledgements

In dedication to all of #teamrockstars and all my lovely Rockstars who have been there with me on the journey so far, to the wonderful Kate Spencer for her unwavering friendship and support, to Steve Bellamy for giving me Wednesday nights to work & Kat Reynolds for taking my vision for the original brand and birthing this awesomely technicoloured and funky brand and to Vicki Nicolson for nurturing the brand and continuing with it's growth (of which we speak more about later). This book is dedicated to all the Rockstars I've ever worked with – you are my inspiration, to inspire me to be more, help more and to do my thang, no matter what.

CONTENTS

Introduction

Chapter 1   What is a Rockstar?....................................1

Chapter 2   Build a Rockstar Brand............................11

Chapter 3   Stand out like a Rockstar.....................31

Chapter 4   Get Famous like a Rockstar..............39

Chapter 5   Rockstar Confidence............................53

Chapter 6   Think like a Rockstar...........................61

Chapter 7   Market like a Rockstar........................89

Chapter 8   Rockstar Products...............................125

Chapter 9   Launch like a Rockstar......................149

Chapter 10   Make Money like a Rockstar...........165

Chapter 11   How to Build a Rockstar Team........181

Chapter 12   Rockstar Tips.......................................187

Chapter 13   Where You Need to Go Pro..............257

More Stuff & Bonus Links.................................261

About Emma...263

✦ INTRODUCTION ✦

Let me take you into a little story. This is the story of how this book came about and how it was birthed into the world. This book is a significant part of my business evolution. It came as a result of My Project 100k. It was a personal project, a target if you like. It was a rally cry to myself to cut through the stuff in business that just simply didn't sit right with me and it was a project that was to stretch my biz building skills and gave me an end point to aim towards. My Project 100k started 12 months before I started writing this book.

What is My Project 100K? It was 12 months, with one mission and one result. I was going to spend 2015 proving that I could bring together a 100k business. The result? I either could or I couldn't. Pretty cut and dry – right?! I do love a challenge and whilst building my business has never been about the money I felt that a financial target and proof that you could grow a business without compromising on your ethics and beliefs was a pretty good challenge to keep me focused.

The result? It was a success.

The whole journey through the 12 months is the subject of another book but the lessons I learned along the way give the foundation and structure that you need in order to be a Rockstar biz owner; the framework upon which to build a successful business without compromising yourself.

The brand continued to evolve.

I wanna hold my hand up and make a bit of an admission – I do not identify myself as a coach, I'm not a fucking coach. I have been stumbling over this one for a LONG time now.

I don't ever refer to myself as a coach and I have massive resistance to using that terminology to define myself.

I think that the word coach comes with massive preconceptions. I have spoken with people before who have believed that working with a coach isn't for them because they will be simply asked questions and will work out the answers for themselves and therefore they are simply paying for someone to be a quiz master in their business. I also know that lots of people think that working with a coach means that you are told what to do and that you become the puppet in your business with your coach heading up the role as chief puppeteer. I simply don't fall into either of those camps.

My work is a fusion business development and strategy, self awareness and mindset bolstering and spiritual principles.

Yes, I ask questions and help you to explore what comes up for you. Yes, I will give you action steps and help you to see a clear path. I hold a light up to you, to your business and to the road ahead. I do this whilst holding a safe space for you to explore your individuality within your business and craft bespoke messages and strategies that will work for you and your crowd.

I am a massive advocate of being yourself in business and stripping away the filters that we put in our way.

I work, intuitively, with people at their own pace.

I un-pretzel people and straighten them out when they have tied themselves up in knots.

I will kick your ass and I will give you a big squishy hug – all depends on what you need.

My approach is beyond basic. I help people to really get to the nitty gritty of what their business is all about, what it actually means and how they can project that out into the world like a great big awesome supernova light.

I am not one for us labelling ourselves and have previously written a blog about ditching the labels and whilst I haven't used the label it's still loitered around me.

So I don't identify myself as being a coach and I have no desire to stick any alternative label on there.

My business isn't about my story but in a perverse way it's laced with it – it's not about me but all about what I can/should share with the world. The message and the teachings that I want to share with heart centred and soulful entrepreneurs. The tools that you need to build a legendary business and move beyond ordinary. It's about helping you fast track through the shit and into the sunshine.

The big thing with business development is that you MUST be willing to dance with your shadow AND please know that we all have one – no matter what stage of business we currently occupy.

It's not just a one time only dance either as you'll have to dance with her regularly and you'll have to keep bringing her forth into the light, whilst listening to what she says and learning from her deep and meaningful lessons.

She is you and you are her.

You can only shine as brightly or as long as you are prepared to keep her dancing in the light. She will communicate with you through your thoughts and she impacts on your actions. She sometimes wants you to stay safe and sometimes she wants you to just go "ah fuck it" let's see what happens. She knows the truth but she also tells lies. She's to be observed and pacified and courted and entertained. She's not to be ignored but sometimes you aren't to give her the time of day. Your willingness to dance will translate into your willingness to be, do and have more. It will be the crux on which you embrace your truth and your message. Your light and your dark make you who you are. Your journey fills in the gaps.

Whilst ready to look at those shadows and examine the things that hold us back I want you to reframe them and become solutions focused. Energy going into the shadow only makes the shadow larger – it's time to step into the sunshine.

Business development is about more than strategy. It's about more than funnels, ROI, marketing metric and budgets. It's about being able to bring yourself and therefore your business into a new place. A place of truth and empowerment. A place of doing what it takes but not burning out. A place where you say what you are here to say and stop shying away from your truth. Embrace it, love it, wrestle with it, hissy fit with it and love it deeply – it's real, raw and nothing more.

I'm not telling you all this because I am seeking to simply tell you why I don't define myself as a coach but more the reason why I need to evolve my business to the next place.

Whilst this shit remains unsaid I am not speaking my truth.

I will never ask you to do stuff that I am not prepared to do myself so I took my own course, I introspected and this is what came out of it.

It's time to move away from the word Coach and variations therefore.

I don't take this decision lightly because my business name

includes the word Coach (Coaching Rockstars) or should I say it did.

We now move forth as Rebels and Rockstars. Nothing else changes but I can free myself from the resistance that I feel around the word and share my message with ease. Resistance keeps us stuck and if you take nothing more from this introduction take the fact that you need to examine the stuff that keeps you stuck.

I am not here to knock Coaches or Coaching but simply say that it's not for me and I don't identify myself with those words. This isn't in any way discrediting the industry of coaching nor is it here to make you wobble about being a "coach." I am totally open – if you totally love being a coach and coaching and that's what runs through your veins then that's absolutely epic! I am here to support you to grow and develop that business. I'm merely making the admission that word/label (whatever you want to call it) doesn't fit right with me.

My business is all about helping you to achieve the next level in your business, it's beyond the basics (but we do make sure you have those firm foundations too), it's beyond ordinary (in fact it's about you creating something extraordinary). It's soulful, it's nourishing, it enhances your mood, fills your cup and helps you ignite that fire in your belly. There are no rules and no labels. There are no secrets. You can be whoever you are because this is about creating a business with your own rules, made by you, broken by you (if you want to). I don't do cookie cutter advice and one size doesn't fit all.

Inspiring | Motivating | Empowering | Strategy | Self Awareness | Biz Awareness | Fulfil Your Potential.

My work is about creating a ripple – if I can help you and you can go on change your world, what the world looks like for your family/friends/acquaintances and how you show up in the world AND you then go on to help more people then we have achieved the beginnings of one AMAZING ripple!

What this book is all about is taking your knowledge, skills and know-how and turning it into a business that is A-MAZING. I am going to show you how you can transform your business into a Rockstar business. A BIG business which makes a difference in the world (and in your world) AND makes money.

I am not prissy about what you call yourself either. If you are selling your knowledge or services then it might be that you have questioned whether you're really c coach? I see arguments about the subject all the time. I see judgment being cast and labels being stuck on people. I couldn't give a shit what you label yourself with. It doesn't matter whether you label yourself as a coach, a mentor, a trainer, a teacher, a cheerleader – it's fine. It matters not! There are more important things in the world to get angsty over.

I'm talking to you if you are a coach, a trainer, an educator, a teacher, a mentor, an adviser OR if you are someone who has knowledge or skills that others would love to learn. It doesn't matter to me which badge you want to wear.

I'm talking to you if you're someone who is on a mission to help other people. The heartbeat of your business is about enabling, educating and helping others. Taking your knowledge, skills, experience and desire to teach other people how to make your world a better place.

It really doesn't matter what you call yourself as long as your calling is to serve your audience. This ain't about get rich quick stuff. This is about living your purpose, serving others and making a bloody good income out of it along the way.

As I said, I'm not here to teach you how to be a coach. I have no formal coaching qualifications but I have a wheelbarrow full of experience and I have learnt lots along the way. I have not been adverse to rolling up my sleeves and making the decision to try new tactics, work with a new strategy and observe what others are doing to make their online business better. I have soaked up knowledge. I have worked with and observed wonderful leaders.

I suppose what I'm saying is that no previous experience is necessary and no formal qualifications are required. Whether you have a big business teaching and supporting others, a business with masses of potential or an idea that's all still in your head right now, this book is for you.

If you want to reach your potential then it's time to stop asking for permission, stop getting in your own way, stop over-thinking. It's time to start doing. It's time to be a Rockstar. Most people only ever operate at a minuscule of their potential and this kinda makes me sad. I want you to step outside of that and I want you to be different. Normal and ordinary isn't a place for you to be!

It's time to allow your ideas to collide. When you allow this your consciousness changes. You become open to possibilities. You hitch up your sassy pants and become willing to see and act on that possibility. If you don't grow and develop then you are going to stay stuck. The journey is fluid. It never ends, you continue to strive further and grow more.

My little girl is a sensitive soul on the inside and whilst watching

Disney films I will often look over to her and see that she's got a tear in her eye.

I have given her a little mantra (and t might work for you too) "If it's not happy, it's not the end."

The possibilities for you and your business are limitless but only if you let them be. If you combine doing the right things and thinking the right way you have the scope to become a Rockstar.

If you limit you, it limits you.

Emma x

1 WHAT IS A ROCKSTAR?

Aaaaahhhh, I'm glad you asked – what on earth is a Rockstar? Why are they different?

This isn't about building an ORDINARY business. If you wanna be ordinary and average that's fine but perhaps you bought the wrong book. Rockstars are an incredible breed of biz owners.

It's someone who is COMPLETELY rocking their brand and getting their business out there in a big way.

A Rockstar is brave and courageous. They will put themselves at the forefront and be prepared to stand in the limelight. Eeeeekkkkkk, you might not feel like that right now. You might feel like you'd much prefer to hide under the nearest rock and not bob your head above that place of safety. That's ok! We can work through that. This book is about giving you practical things that you can do in order to embrace the fire in your belly. The bravery comes in acknowledging that actually building this business isn't about you. It's time to ditch the ego and it's time to move into this business being focused on the people you are here to serve.

Biz Rockstars don't hide and they don't just take the comfortable pieces of the puzzle, the stuff that is safe.

That's not to say that the steps that they take are risky. Far from it. It's just that there's a feeling of un-comfort attached to the unknown. They are willing to be brave, to do the stuff that seems scary. In essence they do the stuff that ordinary biz owners daren't do.

They are confident and sassy (don't worry if you don't feel that way right now, we'll get that sorted!!).

It took me a little while. I took the polite and comfortable bits. I played safe. I did average stuff and got average results. I sprinted along, at times, in my business without very much thought about everything. Those bits that stretched me, yeah sure, I took those on, for a little while. I would implement, start to see results and then it would just fall by the wayside. I would shrink back into my comfort zone.

When the mission in your business is to help and support other people with their growth and their journey, there is never an exact science to be applied. Business generally is unpredictable. Why do you think that most people have a proper job? You WILL need to be brave enough to try new things. Be patient enough to give them time. Be wise enough to know when it isn't working and be courageous enough to make changes when necessary. It's a fine balance. You need to be stubborn enough to give stuff a proper shot but wise enough to know when stuff needs a tweak!

Definition of "a tweak"

This is when you need to make small changes, vary something. When you need to freshen things up all the way through or turn around and change something in a big way. We can have BIG tweaks and LITTLE tweaks. Sometimes there simply needs to be a change in title, headline or words and other times there needs to be a change of topic or subject. Either way, never be afraid of the tweaks!

Very often when you get stuck in your biz you beat yourself up. I know that at times you feel a rippling of regret, regret that you didn't do things differently, that you made mistakes. Do you want to continue the self-beating about each and every one of them or are you ready to forgive yourself and move on?

It's ok! Everyone makes mistakes and everyone clings to that which is comfortable – it's natural. Everything we do shapes the way that we build our business, with every "mistake" we gain more knowledge, more to teach our crowd. The lessons will be constant. The journey maketh the biz owner.

I love this quote.

> 66
>
> "In life we do things. Some we wish we had never done. Some we wish we could replay a million times in our heads. But they all make us who we are. And in the end they shape every detail about us. If we were to reverse any of them we wouldn't be the person we are. So live, make mistakes, have wonderful memories, but never second guess who you are, where you have been and most importantly where it is you're going."
>
> *Carrie Bradshaw*

My Project 100k came as a result of lots of experience. I am not sitting here and selling you an overnight success. I'm not saying that if you opened a business today, without any experience or any audience, then you will suddenly skyrocket into a 100k business. I know that you are only a failure if you stop trying and give up. Instead, learn the lessons and move forwards. Do you know something? You don't even have to want a 100k business. We will talk about that in a mo!

It may be that you will never be satisfied. In fact, scrub that, a Rockstar WILL never be satisfied. You will always be ready for the next challenge. Just as you are approaching that goal, you will already have the next one up your sleeve. You are unlikely to give yourself any credit, whatsoever, for what you have achieved. Your current achievement won't be enough in your eyes. You're likely to be your biggest, strongest and loudest critic.

I bet there are times when you have said... I'll tell you what I'll do. I'll work harder, I'll push more. I'll hustle. I'll stare at my bloody computer screen for a few more hours...

Just waiting.

What for?

I've no idea – but I know I won't miss anything.

I'll then probably get a little sweary. Cue a little self-assault – why are you wasting your time, not moving forwards blah blah blah...

I'll take a look at what others are doing. I'll unleash the dirty great green-eyed monster of jealousy and envy and think – ack, how come they can do it and not me?! You'll never have a business like (insert your favourite biz inspiration here). (FFS!! You know that these thoughts definitely don't serve you BUT they still arrive!)

Why can't I make this work?

I'm so far behind.

I'm so stuck.

I'm so lost.

I can't.

I won't.

I shan't.

Balls, perhaps I should just give up and stay safe. Is it time to cut my losses and get a "proper" job?

Does it have to be hard?

Yes and No!

Usually it has to be hard until you work out that it doesn't have to be hard. It's a little like an initiation ceremony. You need to REALLY want it! Most people stop when it feels hard. Success is usually just around the corner but they've already turned back.

If you are serious about growing your business then now's the time to don your Rockstar persona – hand me the keys to your comfort zone (you can take your comfort blanket with you in case you need it but you need to leave the zone behind). Have a farewell party if you like.

It's time to become a leader.

It's time to show your fans that you're serious about helping them, that you're the right person for them. It's down to you now, it's time to go pro!

I ain't going to shout and swear at you. I ain't going to "call you out". I'm certainly not going to tell you that it's my way or not at all. For me it's much different. There are lots of shouty coaches out there but I ain't one of them, it's not my style!

Confession Time

Sometimes I make my lovely clients cry, it's not something I'm proud of nor is it something I seek out but it's often where the shift starts. Inevitably it brings a realisation, it releases the stuff that's stuck, it brings about A MASSIVE change. It takes them out of their comfort zone. It makes them realise their current position. Face up to it almost. It's often the case that they aren't truly doing what they should be doing. Something shifts.

The questions that often bring about the biggest revelations are:

Do you love your business in its current state? Right now, today, does it make your heart sing? There is absolutely no point scaling up and building a business that you do not love.

How is your boss to work for? Are you the worst boss in the world? If you had a boss like you in an employed role would you be bitching about her at the water cooler?

Once the shift occurs they become ready.

In the quiet contemplation the passion rises and sometimes with passion comes a vulnerability. Excitement and fear combine. It's a giddy mix. It can often be an absolute rollercoaster of emotions. It can be exhausting at times. You may feel vulnerability that if you "put yourself out there" that the impact might not be as you had hoped. A feeling of lying naked (not literally but in a baring your soul kinda way).

It's not roary or shouty. It's a stirring, a re-ignition of the fire in your belly, tingly toes and heartbeats of fear – but in a good way.

Then the door is open to be pragmatic. We can't change that which is gone.

We have no time to look back.

It's time to turn your attention forwards. It's time to do what you REALLY need to do.

It's passion, it's integrity, it's bravery, it's pride. Now is the time to harness it and make the future different.

Turn off the stereo and tap into the heartbeat of your business.

Let's dive into what you can do to make that difference now....

THE 100K THING.

I wanna nip back and examine this bad boy!

Ah, the old 6 figure business malarkey!

Is it the definition of success?

Is it the benchmark of business?

Am I supposed to dream of it?

I am writing this having achieved a 6 figure business and having been in the position to grow my business in the MOST amazing way.

I have harnessed my passion and built a business which has NEVER felt icky or aggressive and which has served lots of soulful and heart centred entrepreneurs around the world. Am I proud of it?- ABSOLUTELY. Do I love it as much today as ever? TOTALLY.

My business is an absolute passion and whilst I work with targets and look after the financial health of my business it's not the be all and end all of why I do what I do. My business is fuelled and driven by passion, it's about being able to help the people I am here to serve. It's not lame to say that business is about more than just the money. It's not a line simply spoken by the unsuccessful.

BUT, what if you don't have any dream or desire to build a 6 figure business - what if you couldn't think of anything worse? Does that mean that you aren't really "in business" and you are just playing around?

NO!!! It doesn't. There's no standard benchmark for where success lies! There's no magic figure that says that once you hit that then you become successful. Success has a very personal definition and it's totally subjective as to where your success point lies. It might be that you want to earn enough money to pay your bills, to live comfortably and to be happy. It might be that you want to change the world - whatever hits your passion points is fine, wherever you find your definition of success - that's fine too.

You don't need to hold on to someone else's dream.

You need to hold yours and hold it tight.

Moving on to one that we see A LOT.

There's a massive marketing movement that talks about overnight success and the fact that you can earn a gazillion pounds a week by working 3 micro seconds per day and only 1.2 days per week. There's a whole tabloid feel to it, sensationalised and provocative approach that is seeking to trigger you into a yearning desire to reveal these secrets – are they even a thing?

In my experience most overnight success stories have a huge back story.

The success came as a result of months, years and perhaps even decades of work which paved the way. Yes, you can experience massive business growth quickly but you have to be in a position to court that movement and to go with it. You have to have done the groundwork to allow that to happen and you have to have the systems and strategies in place to work with the growth. The business successes I have seen have been timely in the making, they have made mistakes along the way and the very best successes have certainly used those mistakes as lessons to help and support other people from making the same decisions or ending up in the same circumstances.

Moving on to the whole making money without working.

Lots of people like to refer to it as "passive income" (gosh that term really pisses me off!). Yes, as you step into your success and after you put all of the hard work in behind the scenes there is an opportunity to not work quite so hard. You will hopefully have refined your systems and built a team around you which will help you to sustain that growth. That will mean that you won't need to be at the coalface quite so much. It will mean that you will be able to step back a little from the grind. I know what it's like when you are doing it all yourself. When you feel really protective over every aspect of your business and don't want to hand over any of the reins to anyone else. It's normal. If you are there right now then please do know it's totally normal – BUT you do need to move beyond that and know that it will ultimately serve you to build a successful team around you and let in a few people in order to help and support you.

You have to put the work in, in order to be a master of your destiny and to lay the success foundations upon which you can build!

CHAPTER REMINDER CHECKLIST

Rockstars is for INCREDIBLE biz owners prepared to build legendary businesses.

No excuses allowed from this point onwards.

It's time for you to mcke your shift.

Forward is the only direction you're travelling.

Let's tap into the heartbeat of your business!

2 BUILD A ROCKSTAR BRAND

A brand is so much more than the name of your business or your logo.

Let's look at some questions...

What is it that you do?

I mean, what do you really do?

What impact do you make on the lives of others?

If you already get niching and exactly the type of work that you do, you might answer this with, "Oooo, I'm a careers coach for women" or "I help therapy businesses to grow their business" or something of the like.

Earlier this year I asked myself this question – what is it that really do? I mean REALLY? How do other people perceive me? I had been helping and supporting biz growth for a while (jeez, see how I avoided the "c" word there – I really dislike that word) for a while and I knew that the women who worked with me and implemented what I taught them got the most amazing results BUT I felt that I had turned a little vanilla. I'd had that feeling

11

on and off throughout the year. I was not connecting with my fans the way that I would have liked to and I was not able to attract new fans into my customer base. Those who worked with me where absolutely stonking their sales and building their businesses MASSIVELY but I wasn't having the impact I wanted to have.

I knew that my brand was starting to strangle me a little bit and it was keeping me boxed in.

I wasn't able to express my true personality and vibrancy through that brand and I was feeling quite claustrophobic. It wasn't a nice feeling.

I asked myself the question – so what is it that you actually do? I scribbled some notes about the things I taught and the results that my clients were seeing but I felt that it wasn't quite enough.

So, what did I do? I asked other people. I got an external perspective of what it was that other people viewed as my strong points, my zone of genius.

I asked a couple of my 1-2-1 clients, my VA and a couple of ladies I worked with in my programmes.

The responses I got from the simple question – "what am I good at" provided me lots of clarity.

I had been very much focused on the practical stuff I shared with my crowd. The masses of "how to" content that was readily available to them. In reality my strengths were much more than that. My strengths included identifying what other people were good at, helping them to get out of their own way, accountability, showing them how to develop their brand, showing them how to stand taller (not bad when you only knock in at 5ft 1in) than the other biz owners in their niche, being supportive, PLUS I can spot wobbles a mile off. It was a much more whole business approach than I had been giving myself credit for. I love helping my clients practically – I knew I wanted to be much more than "theory". I wanted to ALWAYS encourage implementation and action and not let the "don't know how" stop people from achieving their potential.

My challenge to you is to start to identify exactly what it is that you do. Start internally and ask yourself the question, jot down your answers, take notes (without filter – shameless book plug – you could always get an "I'm A Flippin Rockstar - The Journal to write it all in), allow it all to come out and down onto paper. Then you must ask AT LEAST 3 other people and allow their answers to provide you with a rounded opinion and the clarity that may not as readily come from within.

So, I briefly touched on the fact that I felt that my brand had started to strangle me and that I had become vanilla. Vanilla is something I am not. I have been told on more than one occasion "you're weird, but I love you". My Valentine's Day Card from my husband even hit me up with the message "you're weird but I like it." (I'm kinda getting the message.)

My brand wasn't allowing me to show my fans the real me. The technicolour me.

I had fallen foul of a trap that I advise my clients on (oooo my gosh, aren't we as business owners so bloomin' good at dishing out the advice and not so good at looking at it within our own businesses?).

Anyhaps, I had been speaking to a client who had effectively been hiding behind her brand. She had kept her brand in front of her face and was ducking down behind it as a safety blanket. She had started to recognise that she was doing this. She even realised that her brand name had absolutely no connection whatsoever with what is that she does. She wasn't even an "exactly what it says on the tin" kinda brand. She was now just hiding.

I encouraged her to be brave.

I encouraged her to stand out in front of this brand and to be herself. She changed her business name to her own name, she changed her website to her own name and she ran with the re-brand AND OH MY GOSH what a difference.

Here's the thing – when you are helping and supporting people on their journey then these people are investing in you. They are deciding whether or not YOU are the right person for them to work with. They need to feel like you are their BEST and SAFEST option. It's kinda like YOU are the right person for them at the right time and you will be able to help & support them in the right ways. You can't hide. You need to be fully, gloriously and unapologetically yourself. Some people will love you, some people will hate you and whilst initially the thought of not being liked is uncomfortable you have to have the Marmite effect. People disliking you isn't paving the way for trolls or haters – it's just that you aren't for them. You can't be everyone's favourite comfy armchair – you need to be the comfy armchair for your peeps – not too soft, not too hard, JUST RIGHT, Goldilocks. You won't have the impact that you are looking for, the impact that will wow, the impact that will get you more clients. You will just be safe, secure and steady. This is fine if you are satisfied with being average and getting average financial returns. No-one is judging you. This is yours!

So your next Rockstar challenge is...

...to work out whether what you are doing right now is you. Are you showing yourself within your brand? Are you showing up within your work?

The alternative is, are you hiding? Are you trying to stay anonymous? Are you a comfy old chair?

Vanilla isn't going to cut it.

The market gets nosier week by week. You can no longer rest on the fact that you have had a client base in the past. You can no longer reminisce over times gone by. You always need to be attracting new fans into your business.

I know that your mission is to help as many people as you possibly can and you can't do that when you are hiding. You need to shine your light, loud and proud.

So what you do + who you are is a start to defining what your business is all about. It needs to be a perfect combination of the two otherwise there won't be balance. Your business won't be soulful and you won't be creating your genius authentically and with integrity.

Next is your mission. I know that it often sounds quite corporate to think about mission statements etc. I'm not asking you to get all corporate with this one but I want you to think about the over-arching mission in your business.

I asked the question in one of my programme groups and got this fantastic response from the lovely **Vicki Nicolson, Brand Creative...** "To use my powers of creativity, psychic intuition and passion to design distinctive brands that are striking and makes entrepreneurs shine online. It's my mission to make you feel great about your business and empower you to stand tall and be proud of your beautiful business."

Anne Hole of Musical ABC said...
"For every child, at least the under 5s, in the UK to have a quality music education! A very big ask! How? By giving EYFS professionals the skills and confidence to bring music into their setting for at least 5 minutes every day."

Kathy Payne – Natural Health and Fertility Coach...
"Educate women to protect their fertility and hormonal health through life."

Sarah Baker of Therapy Biz Coach said...
"To stop therapists thinking they have to live in poverty or exhausted trying to get local clients when if they learned how to market properly and get online they could have a successful money making business transforming people's lives (which is all they really want to do!)"

For me...

"I want to show you how to grow your business, so that you can help as many people as you can (start the ripple). I want you to own your brand, stand at the top of your field and make money (because money isn't icky). I want to show you that they don't need to be ordinary or average – that they can be Rockstars instead."

Be yourself, unless you can be a Rockstar and then of course make the choice to be a Rockstar!

So let's go on to the way you will have traditionally thought about your brand and that will be your branding. The look and feel of what you do. You may have thought that your brand was all about your logo but it's about MUCH more than that.

What's my brand all about then?

Your brand is about the whole look + feel of your business. It's about colours, fonts, language, style and everything that people will come into contact with. From your Facebook Page to your Pinterest account, your website to your Instagram page and everything in between. There needs to be continuity in your brand. People need to know at a glance that they are in the right place, that they have found YOU and not just another business that looks like you. It needs to be familiar.

Everything needs to work together.

I have had my branding designed by my gorgeous graphic design genius and she has produced some branding guidelines for me. I have seven colours within my brand although tend to only work with five of them. I have three font families I choose from and three logos I work with. All in all that allows me to have a consistent look and feel across my platforms.

I also have a photographer who I work with who finds consistency. Brand Rockstar is about me, my imagery (both of me and the other images I use within my business), the design work on printables and other business assets as well as my website.

Every piece blends together to create a harmonious look and feel to my brand.

The final piece in the branding puzzle is the language I use both orally and in text. I have always taken an informal approach to my language. I write as I speak and I speak as I write. It may not always be the Queen's English but I don't care, the grammar police DO NOT keep me awake at night. I spent years in corporate world writing in "proper" English, including old English and Latin (it bored me rigid), so I decided early on that I needed to ensure my personality came across in my words when I started my business.

Let's just touch on swearing too! I avoided it initially in my business. I used words like "ruddy" and "jolly well" and "two hoots". Oh my woolly word – that's so not me! I have a heart of gold but the language of a sailor at times. As I was hiding that I wasn't being true to myself and can you imagine the incongruence if people then came to work with me and I got a bit sweary with them? Now I'm not swearing like a trooper or for effect but sometimes no other word will do!!

Continuity and consistency is the name of the game within your brand's look and feel.

There is a light which shines brightly right at the centre of your brand. That light is the epicentre of your brand. That light is your fans. Your fans need to be that core and you need to start to understand them.

To get inside their heads.

To feel as if you are walking in their shoes.

I WANNA TAKE YOU ON MY BRAND EVOLUTION

Brands, branding, look & feel – all that jazz!

Is it important? What does it even mean?

What do you need to be thinking about?

When you first start out in business you are super fixated on logos. I know that I certainly was. The logo was the important thing. But brands are about much more than logos.

The other thing to know is that brands evolve. If you are waiting until you have the perfect logo before you get started then stop that search. I promise it's nowhere near as important as you think it is at the very beginning BUT getting your whole brand right really is.

So, I wanna introduce you to clenched (& still quite corporate) Emma from her first photoshoot and branding.

The Launch Queen brand was super beautiful. I was designed by Leanne from Jakenna Design It's elegant and opulent. It's stunning. I loved the little magical swish underneath it.

BUT the brand kept buffering up against me. It was a brand which was absolutely gorgeous, it simply wasn't me!

I was stuck in it. I was stuck using blacks and golds/yellows within my imagery. I was stuck with photos that weren't versatile enough to add any additional layer of personality on to the brand.

It felt like I'd cornered myself into a black & gold corner and there was no getting out.

I remember scraping the money together to get those photos done. It seems like I got lost in my former corporate days when I look back at them now. They are super staged (yup I look younger and thinner) BUT they don't should my eclectic personality.

I had evolved.

My confidence & trust in myself had evolved.

I didn't need to hide in black.

AND really – that necklace isn't me at all!!

Time to re-brand.

Time to unclench a little (just like I advise my Rockstars to – see I know because I've been through the process).

Ah, already a lot more me!!

A photoshoot in the beautiful Newcastle Upon Tyne and a rebrand – therein was born Coaching Rockstars.

The brand is beautiful and was designed by the gorgeous Kat from The Business Beautician.

BUT the evolution continued. I think that when you first step into your business properly you have all sorts of ideas about what it needs to look like and how it needs to be. You will be guided on the evolution of your brand by your crowd and by the projects you undertake and how things need to look.

Queue further evolution into Emma Holmes – Coaching Rockstars...

I was working with the gorgeous Vicki Nicolson – Brand Creative with the design work generally within my business. We needed a more versatile library of images. We needed to show my normality, my fun, my tell-it-like-it-is but smothered with compassion, love & light. We needed imagery to use on my new website, in my books and on social media.

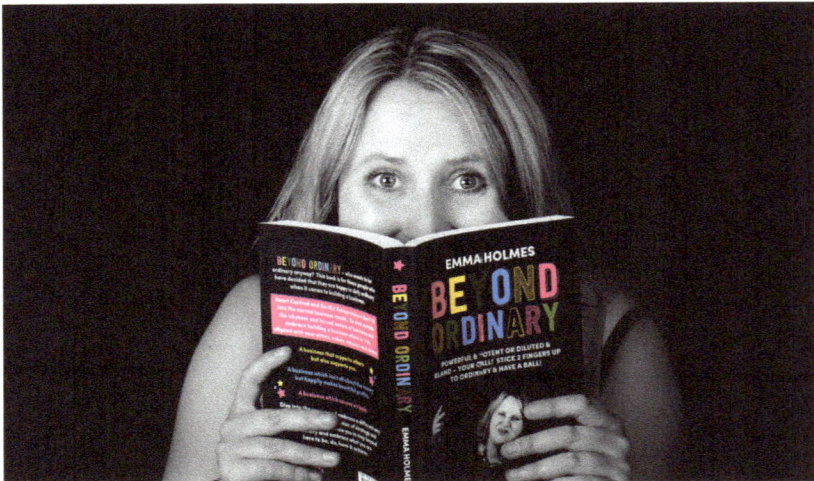

Then the final evolution to take us where we are today was to embrace the new name – Rebels and Rockstars and ditch that "coaching" tag once and for all!

Why have I done it?

Because at each stage it's felt right. It's felt like the action that needed to be taken. I have found an amazing photographer and we have committed to regular shoots with the gorgeous and talented Natasha Holland. Is that because I'm vain? Is it because I can't settle on pictures? No, it's because they are super important in my overall brand. They are fun. They give a sense of who I am and what I'm all about. They save money and time wasted searching stock photography. They are different because no-one else can be me and use my images. I have an expressive face and we have stacks of fun doing them.

I'm sure you'll agree that you get much more of a sense of who I am from the later pictures than the earlier ones.

My advice?

Don't be afraid to change.

Don't be afraid to include lots of personality into your brand as that is what makes you unique – no-one can serve your audience like you do!

Get good images as they will set you free.

YOUR BRAND IS NOTHING WITHOUT THE FANS IT SERVES.

You need to know what makes them tick, what they are worried about, what they struggle with and what you can do in order to impact upon their world. This epicentre is your service point. Your brand needs to resonate with your fans. As a Rockstar you'll never sell Heavy Metal records to an audience of Classical Music buffs. It's the same for you. You need to surround yourself with people who "get" what you do, who are interested to find out more and who are the perfect people for you to serve.

An interesting one that I hear a lot of the time is a question that surrounds selling – how do I sell my programme to people when they don't know they need it. You don't!! Either your fans know they want it and will buy it because it will help them to get unstuck, or you have the wrong fans right now or you have the wrong programme OR you have totally got your message wrong. Your fans will get what you offer (as long as you are explaining it properly).

It's easy to find out more about your fans when you interact with them but if you are seeking clarity about your audience before you have any direct access to your fan base then you need to be a little more creative.

My suggestion is to still ask them but you need to do this in a more public way. Public for you not for them. We're not talking about baring souls in public! Put the question out there on social media or put together a survey.

I know that at times it's easy to disconnect with your crowd, people do it a lot. You can forget what it's like to NOT know the things that you know. You can be left second guessing what it is that they need help with, you can blindly stab about in the dark.

My Challenge to you is to start to bring together a Raving Fans Notebook – this is a concept I've used for a while now with my clients and I also use it personally within my business.

27

What on Earth's a Raving Fans Notebook, Emma?

I'm pleased you asked that. A Raving Fans Notebook is where you keep all the details about your fans in one place. It's where you can refer back to when you're stuck and you need to re-connect with your audience.

- Write words and phrases about what your audience are stuck with, their biggest problems, the things that are like little viruses in their head.
- Write words and phrases about where they would like to be, their dreams, their goals, their aspirations.
- Things they struggle with.
- How they feel.
- Emotional triggers.

Get it all down on paper. It's also a perfect excuse to buy a beautiful notebook because you are going to refer back to this one all of the time. You can add to it as your fan base grows and you get to know them better too (this notebook is worth the investment).

As time goes on and people ask you more and more questions you can keep adding to this truly valuable resource.

I have put together a video about how to bring together an amazing raving fans notebook in the free resources that accompany this book – access it here >>>

www.beabusinessrockstar.com

YOUR ROCKSTAR CHALLENGE...

Get that Raving Fans Notebook on the go!

Check in with your consistency of your brand – make those little tweaks where necessary (know that you don't have to go all out on a rebrand, those little ways of achieving continuity will make a massive difference).

... it's time to reflect on what it is that you're missing right now. Take some time to study the beginnings of your crowd notebook and see where the gaps are in your business right now (there might be gaps in your blogs or your products or your freebies).

Here is the calculation:
What You Do + Who You Are + Your Look & Feel + Your Fans + Continuity & Consistency = A Rockstar Brand

And remember...

"Your Brand Is the Single Most Important Investment You Can Make In Your Business."

Steve Forbes

3 STAND OUT LIKE A ROCKSTAR

We've touched on how hiding just won't cut the mustard and in order to stand out there is no way in this world you can do it whilst hiding. You can't attract lots of people to work with you and get to know your brand whilst you are peeking out of the side of a cushion – FACT.

I know it can be scary.

I know that you feel open to being judged.

I know that there is a vulnerability that sneaks up on you.

Let's get this one out of the way straight off – not everyone is going to like you, not everyone is going to like what you do. Not everyone is going to resonate with your message and do you know what? That is fine, no, actually, it's better than fine – that's AWESOME.

You can't be all things to all people.

You can't be safe and only court the polite little pieces of the puzzle. You are going to have to stand out. This will feel a little uncomfortable at first but please rest assured that it's not that this place is unsafe, it's just the un-comfort of growth!

Blending in isn't good for business.

It can feel incredibly scary when you consider that people may not like you BUT you're all grown up (whether you act it or not) and you can handle it. It'll all be ok. What's the worst that can happen? One of my most favourite quotes touches on this one....

66

"Don't be distracted by criticism. Remember - the only taste of success some people have is when they take a bite out of you."

Zig Ziglar

Okay, you've spent the last chapter looking at what it is you're all about, so now you're ready for this one. You are ready to create a message that you can be loud and proud with. You know what your business missions are and your mission.

You need to inject your personality into your business. This will not only make your business copy-proof as no-one else can be you BUT it will also allow you to stand out.

You don't need whacky hair or an amazing wardrobe to do this. You don't need to be stick thin or look a certain way. But, equally, it's fine if you do too.

You just need to show up and be YOU in every glorious way.

People connect with people. People form relationships with people and relationships are a MASSIVE part of your business.

You need to form relationships with your fans.

THEN nurture those relationships.

Standing out like a Rockstar is one of the easiest things (but the scariest thing) that you can do in your business. It's all about you being you. Unapologetically you. You don't need to change anything, you just need to come out as yourself. You need to break down the barriers and reconnect with the real you. You don't need to filter yourself with the "professional" filter. You need to show people how you can really help them.

How can you be doubly different? I am not talking about changing your appearance and becoming all "whacky" here either (but if you are a little whacky that's cool). What I am talking about is taking a look at the market place. This is not an exercise for you to beat yourself around the head with. I don't want you saying, "Aahhhhh but she's prettier and thinner and younger than me" OR "She's more polished than I am".

I want you to look objectively (and if you struggle with this then enlist some family or friends as moral support).

This is a little project to undertake BUT only when you are feeling super strong and in a good place. If you are feeling a little wobbly then avoid this one until a day where you feel much more resilient. Who are the other people that your fans are likely to be following? Write a little list of other Facebook pages or websites that they are visiting. Take a look at their social media feeds. It'll start to give you an idea of what your fans' feeds will be filled with. What are the newsfeeds of your fans likely to look like? What kinda images are being used and what information is being shared?

What lines are they being fed?

I know that in my industry, my fans are getting really bored of #1 secret, ninja technique blah blah blah to make zillions overnight and only work 36 minutes per month. It's boring now. People are catching on to the marketing speak. Yes, it will always attract attention BUT my fans are so over it. I know that these headlines unleash the curiosity beast inside and that people worry they are missing out but in the cold light of day my fans know that this marketing is simply feeding them marketing speak to get their attention. They are perhaps untruths, half-truths, unattainable expectations – whatever!

As a side note - there is no MASSIVE secret that you are missing out on!!

How can you be a breath of fresh air in your industry? What can you do differently? Take inspiration from outside of your industry too. I often spend time looking at websites and social media accounts which are completely unrelated to my sector. What lessons can you learn there? What inspiration can you gain from what others are doing?

OK – I don't want to miss this one out here. Inspiration is exactly that. It's about taking what you have seen and learnt and being inspired by it. Looking at ways that you can use the concept in your business. It's not about taking the exact same concept and copying it. Copying ain't cool. Don't try to dress copying up as inspiration either. I have had many things blatantly copied and also "inspired" stacks too. I have read my posts and emails delivered by others. I have thick skin now BUT it's still not cool.

Your next step is to do the stuff that others daren't do.

What is it that makes you and your peers quake in your boots? What is it that you would do if you lost weight, didn't have a funny accent, transformed into a princess?

Whatever those things are (and often it's about videos, investing in your business or investing in coaching – sssshhh) then now's the time to do them. Now's the time to buckle up, unclench and get in front of the camera, if that's your nemesis .

One of the most important things I did to stand out in my business was to go pro. It was to start to invest in my business. It was about getting my website overhauled professionally and making that investment in my web presence. It was about getting the support I needed to grow my business. It was about getting professional photo shoots done and professional videos recorded. It was about investing in the tech that made my life easier.

It was really about taking things seriously.

It was about slowing down and thinking things through.

Please stop sprinting blindly. This is a sure sign of a young business in panic mode. I see it (and I've done it in the past) people go off and create stuff overnight or they vomit stuff out there that isn't thought through.

Always run a filter through yourself:
- Is this what the CEO of a company would do or is this what (insert the person that inspires you) would do?
- Why are you doing it?
- What is the outcome you hope to achieve?
- Tell me, what's the business objective with this one?

Take your business pro, invest in yourself and your brand presence.

Be brave.

Step up.

Let your fans get to know you. Let a little of your guard down. Everything doesn't need to be super polished but you have to reflect yourself and your brand in the best possible light at all times.

Get it done but get it right.

Stop compromising, stop being cheap.

Standing out is also about giving your fans what they want.

What do your fans want?

What is it that they are struggling with?

Become their go-to person. Be their resource of choice.

Giving your fans what they want will mean that you are standing out. You will be showing them that you "get" them. You understand and that you are here to help them.

I am a big advocate of taking a whole view look at your business. There is room for a mix of marketing and messages, there is room for lots of your personality BUT what you are sharing still needs to be useful. You need to avoid getting sucked into the guff and fluff. You need to truly be of service to your fans.

If you are useful, entertaining, educational, inspiring and solving your crowd's problems THEN they will keep coming back for more.

You need to be the BEST person for YOUR FANS. Not for everyone but the BEST person for your fans.

Claim your spot at the top of your niche. Claim it, live it and become the real "go-to" expert. I have been working with a lady who perceived that she was up against a "celebrity" at the top of her niche. That was until people started to tell her that they were choosing to work with her over that so-called celebrity as they found her stuff more useful, she made more sense and she was the right fit for them.

You need to become their leader and that's how you will stand out.

The calculation is here:
Your AUTHENTIC voice + Bravery + Doing What Scares You + Doing What Others Won't + Taking Your Place At The Top + Serving Your Crowd = Standing out like a Rockstar.

CHAPTER REMINDER CHECKLIST

Blending in is bad for business.

It's time to start doing the stuff others are scared to do.

Start investing in your business so you can
work it like a pro.

Stand out by giving your fans what they want.

Being you – the real you, not the one who's lurking behind
the cushion – will bring results!

4 GET FAMOUS LIKE A ROCKSTAR

A trigger word for lots of people "FAMOUS". Eeeee but I don't want everyone knowing the ins and outs of my everyday life, I don't wanna share every aspect of my very being with the whole. Hold fire, let's go through it...

It's time to get FAMOUS!!! Now, I'm not talking reality TV famous (icky!) here but I'm talking about you becoming famous in your world, in your niche – people will know who you are and what you're all about.

People will be inspired by you and seek you out for advice and assistance. You will be the sought-after keynote speaker at events. You will be a leader in your field. It's important that you are prepared to get yourself out there in a big way with your brand. You need to become famous for what you do.

Have signature programmes and be known for them.

Have people know about you and what you do.

Become referable because people know what your specialism is.

What Do You Do?

Your first step to getting famous like a Rockstar is making sure people know exactly what it is that you do.

This includes your family and friends. I know, I know, your family and friends may never be your clients BUT they will always be your cheerleaders and you don't know when they might come across an opportunity to cheerlead you. This is making sure you don't get caught in the Chandler Bing thing. Let me explain...

There is a classic episode of Friends where Rachel and Monica are seriously contesting the ownership of the best flat (the girls' flat) with Chandler and Joey with a quiz. A long running saga has lead into this of no-one having any idea what it is that Chandler does for a living. Unsurprisingly the flat is lost when the question that arises is "what is Chandler's job?" Silence and flapping ensues. No-one knows! Made up jobs are bandied about.

What does Chandler Bing do for a job?

In case you are interested this is what Google told me – Chandler works as an IT procurement manager with the specialization "Statistical analysis and data reconfiguration" which he takes up as temporary work, and albeit working in the industry for years and thoroughly loathes.

To be honest it's still not a whole lot clearer!

Anyhaps, the thing is that I have been accused of this recently. My brother said to me, "You're like Chandler". I was certainly a little taken aback and unsure what he was talking about. Was he implying I was a little awkward socially or a "try hard, no succeedy" kinda joker. Eeekk – what was he saying? It transpires that he said that no-one in the family really knew what I did. No-one had any idea what my business was all about.

This was a time of me not taking my own advice. Eeeekk!!

Does everyone know what you do?

You never know who will need your help and assistance. According to recent data everyone on Facebook (and there is an awful lot of us now) have about 400 "friends". This network means that the ripple effect of your message can be massive (but only if people know what you do).

How can people refer you to their friends if they have no idea what you do?

Are you even really clear on what you do? (You had better be or else you need to zoom back a couple of chapters!)

I am not talking about you spending time with every member of your family and each and every one of your friends, and taking an age to explain (in intricate detail) exactly what you do. BUT more a broad brush approach to what you do - an elevator type pitch if you like - which will allow them to know whether they should be mentioning you if a conversation arises within their network that you could assist with.

The power of people knowing is that ability to tap into other networks, is to be referable, is to have an unpaid sales force that will help spread the word about you and your business.

If you are really specific in what you do then you become more spreadable. People are able to refer others to you. You become really easy to refer to because people know how you can help others.

So, here goes...

I am Emma Holmes and I help, mentor and advise heart centred and soulful business owners, coaches, mentors, consultants and teachers. I help them to grow fabulous businesses which are aligned with their values and passion, show them how to continue to love and enjoy their business and still make fabulous profits. My zone of genius is taking those lovely clients into a fantastic online leveraged business model, allowing them to work the hours that they want and make the profits that they desire. I mix together a fusion of business strategy, mindset work and spiritual principles and help them to become a leader in their field AND a complete Rockstar.   No compromise.

Your turn....

My Rockstar challenge to you is...

...to write down, in just a paragraph exactly who you serve in your business and what it is that do.

In order to become famous you need to be prepared to do the things that other people aren't prepared to do. You need to be a little bit brave, a little more strategic and get out of your own way much more regularly.

You need to be prepared to shout about what you do.

It's All About Me

You MUST make sure that your "About Me" page on your website articulates exactly what it is that do and has a very personal feel about it. It's an area of your website which often gets written and neglected. This isn't a do it once kinda job and leave forever. I make sure that my "About Me" page is all about me. It's the only time in your business where it's uber important to get right into the "All About Me Mentality" and do a bit of peacocking. Make sure that you are using that About Me page to let your audience know a little bit more about you, let them find out how you came to be doing what you do and get a little bit of insight into your world.

Make sure that About Me page is letting people identify that they are the right people to be helped by you. Have factors which help them to identify themselves as well as showing them the types of problems you solve.

You About sections on your social media pages also need to be fully completed so that if people come across you on then they are able to find out much more about you. I would also like to see you using pictures of you as your social media profile pictures and in your marketing – no hiding behind logos!

Your marketing is integral to get you to become famous like a Rockstar but there are other things that you need to consider too.

PR Like A Pro

PR is a great way of getting yourself in front of a new crowd. Identifying the publications you wan⁻ to be in and your potential fans are likely to read. I see PR as having two strands to it really. There is PR for credibility and PR to be found by your audience.

Recently I have heard more and more people who are selling PR opportunities, ok – so not really selling PR opportunities, but the chance to effectively purchase the logos that they can use in their marketing. A "submit ycur press release and you'll get featured here" kinda package. I find this a little icky and disingenuous. It's a form of trickery. Your fans think you are massively credible because you have some big name media logos and what has happened is that you have purchased a package where your article will gc onto the far reaches of a media website so that you can use their logos – it's not one that sits well with me and works with my integrity to be transparent with my fans. I would rather not use logos in my marketing as buy them – although I still think that PR does masses for your credibility. Just make sure you are coming upon those logos with integrity.

The other type of PR is the sort that will get you in front of your potential fans. For this kind of PR you need to think about the publications that your fans are likely to read and how you can take steps to be featured in there.

Here are some examples of ways you can start to get some PR for your business.
* Firstly you need to think about which magazines or publications you would like to be featured in

- Are they relevant to your fans? (If you are not sure then ask your fans what they read)
- Follow journalists on Twitter
- Follow the hashtags - #jurnorequest, #prrequest and #journorequest
- Set up Google alerts on your niche so that you can find out if people are looking for stories
- **Have a good little bio about you and your business and great photos you can use (I have a media pack – I've popped a link to it in the goodies you can get with this book – www.beabusinessrockstar.com**

If there are particular magazines that you want to be featured in then go out and buy them. You can often get the names of the editors within the magazines but you can also see the types of articles they are featuring.

Try to find out the deadlines that the magazines and publications on your hit list have. You can also ask when the best time to send in a press release is.

You can cover:
- Industry specific topics if the publication is article/ information based
- Comment on news events
- Give information about news in your company
- Share the results of a survey/stats you have compiled that would be of interest to your crowd
- Provide a good news story
- Celebrate a success

You can also include a Media section on your website which lets people feature you quickly and easily. PLUS, give them information on how to get in touch with you to discuss any PR opportunities further. You can include on that webpage your bio, photographs of you and your logo as well as some articles which you have prepared and a list of topics which you can cover. PR isn't just about print publications. You can also think about radio and television. The first time I did television was absolutely, totally and completely terrifying but I decided to jump on in there and do it anyway. I was briefed and mic-ed up and then off I went. As soon as the interviewing started I felt exactly the same as I do during a live webinar and it was like the presenter and I were just there for a chat. If you don't have the time or inclination to spend time chasing media opportunities, then you can outsource this work to someone who specialises in PR. The chances are that they also have pre-established contacts within publications and can get your stuff featured with much more ease than you ever could.

Be My Guest

Another way of getting seen is to be interviewed on other people's podcasts or on their blog. Guest blogging can be an extremely good way of getting you in front of the right audience. You need to look at people who are attracting similar fans to you but who are not in competition with what you do. Approach people and ask them if they would like to do a guest blog swap – you'll be surprised, there will be people out there who are interested. Put together a list of people who you might be interested in collaborating with.

Make sure you think through the type of audience that they have right now and whether or not you would be able to come together as a good match for one another.

With all elements of PR and guesting there's a slight word of caution. Remember that, whether you like it or not, you will have an ongoing association with the businesses that feature you or that you guest for. You don't want to be jumping into bed willy nilly with publications or business owners. Make sure they are that perfect fit.

Stand Up and Be Seen

Speaking engagements are another great way that you can "get famous" within your niche. You can either organise your own speaking events or you can seek out speaking opportunities.

I have done both. I have been approached to do speaking events AND I have also put together my own events where I have done Accelerator Days for my lovely clients.

If you want to get involved in speaking then the first thing to do is to put it out there. Ask on your social media or pop a little bit in an email to your fans to say that you are going to be doing some speaking and if anyone is interested in you speaking at their event or networking group then get in touch.

Speaking events might be local or national or even international.

You can look for speaking opportunities online, you can join the Professional Speakers Association or other networks that encourage speakers.

My top tips when it comes to speaking are:

Seek out speaking opportunities that are going to get you in front of the right audience for you. You can start to dip your toe into speaking with local networking groups. Hone your craft BUT then it's important that you become a little more discerning about your audience because you need to be sure that the audience is right. It's no use you being in front of a lot of local retail businesses if you seek to inspire people who have an online business, or speaking to those who are in the finance sector if you are looking at holistic therapies (of course you can pick up some people along the way BUT it's not the best use of your time).

Remember that speaking takes up a fair amount of your time – factor that into any speaking engagements that you agree to do. You will need to prepare your presentation, practice your presentation, travel to the speaking opportunities, deliver and then travel home again. It can eat a couple of days out of your diary so be sure that it's right! I also find that I am REALLY tired after I have delivered a speaking engagement and I do need a couple of days out of normal routine before getting back to "business as usual".

Here are some ideas for finding speaking opportunities...
- Look at any local networking groups that might be of interest to you. Go along to them, see what they are like, build some relationships whilst you are there, work out if they are the right crowd for you and then offer to speak if it all sits well with you.
- Look at any industry groups within your sector, these

may be regional or they may be national/international. Check them out, see if they are a good fit for you and whether they have speakers at their events. Introduce yourself and offer your services to them.

- Ask your clients if they attend any meetings or events that may be of interest to you or whether they are part of any groups that you could go along and speak at.
- Check out Eventbrite (online events booking system) and Facebook events to see if there are any events that may be of interest to you there.
- To get famous like a Rockstar you are going to have to stand higher, stay taller and do everything you can to be seen.

Market Like A Pro

An important part of getting famous within your niche is to make sure that you are mastering your marketing. Marketing is SUPER important to you getting out there and people knowing exactly what it is that you do. If people don't know that you exist, then they can't become your fans and they can't buy from you. Marketing is an art (not a science) that you will need to master and we cover this fully in a chapter all of its own.

Team Sales

A great way of standing out and being seen is by doing a fantastic job for your clients. When you help your clients to change their world then they become a fantastic, unpaid, sales team within your business. Make sure you are capturing your clients' success, ask for (and use) testimonials and case studies.

People love to get their teeth into a good success story.

More than that, people know that marketing law dictates that you say that your stuff is awesome. Other people backing that up gives you a much more powerful level of kudos.

Partner Up

Another way to get out there and get known is to engage the help and support of some joint venture/affiliate partners. This would involve you coming to an agreement with other people about them being recompensed (or not if they are friends) for promoting your brand.

It's important that you choose any joint venture partners wisely. If these people are promoting you then you need to know that they have an audience that will be interested in what you do. You need to be thinking about people who are marketing to a similar fan base but that their products are not similar to yours. Perhaps they have products or services which would perfectly compliment what you offer. Also, make sure that your business ethics align with that potential partner. Your reputation is important so make sure you only ever partner with the right people.

The great thing about enlisting the help of others is that you get the opportunity to get in front of their crowd and you are doing this with their endorsement, they are saying to their crowd – come talk a look at this, it's great!

Yes, you will need to (more often than not) recompense people for this financially but it's a fab way to cast your net further afield and attract new people into your fan base.

When you are working with others you are getting help – you are turning people into partners.

Approaching potential joint venture partners needs a specific approach. You need to be going out there, not for your own gain, but with the mindset of how you can help the potential joint venture partner and their audience.

Living the Dream

It was a line I used to pull out all the time in the corporate world. "How are you?" I'd get asked. "Living the dream" would always be my response. Dependent upon my tone, that one could cover a multitude of emotions!

But in this instance we are talking about REALLY living the dream!

You also need to be living your brand. You need to attach your face and name to everything that you do.

You need to get known for your "thing".

Here is the calculation for you:

People knowing what you do + media + PR + standing at the forefront of your brand + speaking + mastering marketing + working with others = Getting Famous Like A Rockstar.

I know that when we start to talk about getting famous there will be times when you're not feeling quite so confident anymore. That's why you are going to need Rockstar confidence too...

CHAPTER REMINDER CHECKLIST

Remember...

Clarity – it's time to get clear on what you do AND make sure EVERYONE knows it.

Nail that elevator pitch and your About Me pages and profiles.

PR like a Pro and start investigating speaking opportunities.

Invest in relationship building – guest blogging + affiliates/ joint venture partners = opportunities.

Get ready to live the dream, Rockstar!

5 ROCKSTAR CONFIDENCE

There will be times when you have wobbles, this is normal but a Rockstar knows that wobbles are merely little imposters that sow seeds of doubt in your brain. When you can recognise the wobbles then you are able to stop them escalating. You regain the control. You get back to being in charge.

A Rockstar has confidence in spade-fulls but that doesn't mean that they don't have to grow and expand and feel uncomfortable at times. It doesn't exempt you from the occasional wobble either.

PLUS, when you first set out on your journey it might not be so easy to tap into your own confidence locker. I find that often people need someone else to believe in them first.

I love this quote from *Good Will Hunting*....

> 66
>
> "Some people can't believe in themselves until someone else believes in them first."
>
> *Good Will Hunting*

Don't be scared of failure.

Break your addiction to the norm.

Believe in yourself – you have the power and opportunity to change the world for the better.

The only limits in life are the ones that you create. You can only grow as far as you are prepared to go.

Your comfort zone will try to protect you from being hurt but you have to tune out from it because your comfort zone will keep you small. Your comfort zone will keep you stuck.

> "If you really want to do something you'll find a way. If you don't you'll find an excuse."
>
> *Jim Rohn*

Often, the only thing stopping you is you.

DON'T BLAME THE UNIVERSE

I am a lover of all things "wooo woco" and whilst I believe that there is so much that you can draw into your life and so much can come your way through fate, it doesn't mean that you aren't in charge and you don't have the power to change stuff.

Yes, when things don't go just as you'd like there is always a lesson in there somewhere. Sometimes it's an obvious one and other times it takes some searching out.

Sometimes we use The Universe as our scapegoat – ack, The Universe dealt me a pants hand there!

Things won't work out as well as they could have if:

- You are constantly working and taking no time out. If you are constantly at the coal face, you have no time to take a good look at the whole view of your business. Your creativity gets stifled and your mojo takes a hike. Rest is so under-rated. Stepping back is something that lots of people forget to do. I get it, you're desperate to make it work and you'll do whatever it takes. You'll work longer and longer hours to chase the dream. A word of warning - it's counterproductive. You will get tired, you'll burn out, you'll not make good decisions. (So there!!)

- You are coming from a place of desperation. I know it sounds weird but when you are coming from a place of desperation, then this comes across in what you do. I know this one is easier said than done because when you feel desperate (either to make an impact, to make things work or to make money) then you can't think of anything else but in these times you push away more than you attract. It kinda works like a little self-sabotaging devil on your shoulder. Your decisions aren't always good. Your work has a feel of desperation about it.

- You are not aligned to what you want. I suppose this is a woo woo one but when you say you want something but that brings about massive doubts in your head and you

55

don't ACTUALLY believe that you can make it happen. When you are working you have to work in harmony, to be mindful of your thoughts as much as your actions because you need both in order to make things work. I always say – **if the mind ain't aligned then the action is irrelevant.** You have to think in the right way and do the right things. Without both there will never be a perfect balance. Yes, you'll still have times when you have wobbles (and that's perfectly normal), these feelings will come to you when you are stretching and growing BUT you need to be aligned with the overall aims and objectives, you need to believe in the possibilities. That perfect place will come with a blend of doing the right things and thinking the right way.

- You are playing small. You are cutting corners and not taking your business seriously. You are making decisions based on fear of spending money or time on the things that are important. You don't spend the majority of your time on income generating activities and you get bogged down in the admin. Playing small keeps you small. You might be frightened of putting yourself out there, you might be fear criticism. It might be that you are being cheap with your business and keeping the purse strings tight. I know that when you first start out you won't have a massive marketing budget and it's important that you spend it wisely. Sometimes you have to invest in yourself, in your business and in development in order to reach the next level. Playing small in mindset, in visibility, in the way you treat your business will not make a Rockstar.

Mindset shifts take a little time, they take tapping into, they take reflection and strategy.

The Universe isn't against you - you're just not helping yourself draw in the right stuff. You just have a block in your path somewhere.

You need to be mindful of what you're doing day to day. Your most precious asset is your time. Don't waste it staring at your Facebook news feed, the answers are rarely there.

Look after yourself, take time off, nurture your creativity, do things that make you happy, think more, don't sprint off with ideas (like a good cup of tea they need a little time to brew - or bruise as my little girl would say). You can make this work, I know you can!

66

"The Universe rewards leaps of faith, you know. Sometimes it takes a wee while. Sometimes just a few days. But it always happens."

Leonie Dawson

About 98% of all problems will be solved if you stop over-thinking stuff and just calm the fuck down!!

> 66
>
> "Those who dare to fail miserably can achieve greatly."
>
> *John F Kennedy*

It's unfortunately the case that at times you are going to hit blocks, you are going to come across uncomfortable situations. You can going to feel like you are being criticised. It's not nice. It often feels like a personal attack. It's a difficult one to decipher because it's business, and business is business, but business is also personal when you are a heart centred entrepreneur and you truly care about that which you are creating.

> 66
>
> "There is only one way to avoid criticism.
> Do nothing, stay nothing and be nothing."
>
> *Aristotle*

There is a massive difference between you expanding and moving through your comfort zones than there is in being confident. Don't confuse the two. You can still have stellar confidence but at times feel as if you are stretching and growing and growth is always a little bit uncomfortable. Growth will ALWAYS step you outside your comfort zone and make you feel a little scared and a little vulnerable BUT this is a good thing. If you aren't pushing forwards and growing and developing then you are standing still, you are staying stuck. If you're not prepared to grow any further then you won't go any further.

Confidence isn't about comfort.

Confidence is about believing in yourself, believing in your business and believing in your brand.

It's about thinking the right way and making decisions from a place of clarity and confidence.

It's about you knowing, deep down (right in the pit of your belly), that you can make this work and that you will do what it takes in order to make your business a success. When you want something badly enough you'll always make it happen.

It's about KNOWING that you are doing a good job with your clients and that they are seeing results.

A great confidence booster is to ask, keep and refer back to the testimonials that you have in your business. Testimonials are ace for Rockstar Confidence (as well as AWESOME for your marketing). If you're having a bad day and would rather not face the world and get out of your PJs then take a look back at your testimonials. Take a look back at the difference you are making to the worlds of others.

Remember that you are doing an awesome job.

Confidence will keep you moving forwards and steady the ship.

You know you have got this covered.

Believe that you can tackle anything that comes your way AND always ask yourself "what's the worst that can happen?"

CHAPTER REMINDER CHECKLIST

Remember...

Recognise those wobbles for what
they are and keep them in check.

To believe in yourself – you have
the power to change the world.

Don't blame The Universe.

Confidence is about believing in yourself.

Keep that testimonial pile building up – it'll help you
through those days where it all feels a bit much and a
result would be getting through the day in one piece, and
a double bonus if you managed to get dressed!

6 THINK LIKE LIKE A ROCKSTAR

You're on a little bit of a journey, because you are your biggest asset but simultaneously you can be your very worst enemy.

You can be the difference between making it or not, you can stand directly in your own way or you can move out of the way and that the path of become smoother, so this is not about you being positive all of the time, this is not about your work life and your home life and your whole life all been Pixies and unicorns because, quite frankly that doesn't happen alright, nobody in the whole wide world is always, always, always in that tip top mindset, but what we need to be doing is looking at getting you into a passively good mindset so that most of the time you've got a great mindset, there will be times where you will feel meh there will be times where you'll feel you know 'I can't believe I'm doing this, and the self-talk fairy on your shoulder, will talk much more about her in a minute, but there will be times where you aren't invincible, there will be times where you feel a little bit meh,

But we are looking at having a passively good mindset most of the time, this isn't about faking an exterior of positivity, we are looking at how you can actively manage your mindset, how you can increase your mindset and how your mindset can effect so much of your business, this is the biggest change you can make

61

in your business, and this will have the most impact on the way that you work on your profitability on the way that you serve your clients on absolutely everything in your business and it is absolutely free for you to implement.

So, we will go through and we will look at how it affects you, look at the things you could be doing in order to step up and change what you have go going now.

Getting Your Head In The Right Place

You need to carve out time to be productive. You need to make sure that you are doing the stuff that's important and that will build your business. You won't create a big business if you are constantly chasing your tail and exhausted.

You need to have a long term strategic plan to move your business forwards. This doesn't need to be boring or set in stone. This is "big picture" stuff that will keep you on track.

What do you want to do in your business??

- Make a certain amount of money?
- Work 1-2-1?
- Leverage your time?
- Be More Visible?
- Speaking?
- Videos?
- Podcasting?
- Blogging?
- Writing?
- Why are you doing this?

What's the BIG reason for doing what you're doing and what difference can it make in your life too?

What If..........

You might be asking yourself "BUT what if I get found out?"

That's a really common one, a lot of people have that imposter syndrome, that they fear that somebody will come to them and go actually, 'do you know what you're not an expert, and you're not telling people the right thing and your products are pants... and and and' so lots of people have that question in what if I get found out.

They also have "what if people don't like me?"

And I know that we all want to be liked at some level, even those that have the 'I don't care what people thinks' you know some people you do care about what they think and it's about making sure your attracting the right sort of people into your crowd, and that you don't care what the other people think, you don't care what the neigh-sayers or the bubble busters or the dream stealers have to say, what if nobody buys?

Well even if you are psychic on these occasions this is your ego! Ok, this is your ego saying 'what if nobody buys? What if what if... nobody can buy ANYTHING from you? When you aren't putting your genius out there, whether that's product, whether that's services, whether its online, whether it's in real life, whatever it may be, if you are not offering that product you are stealing from the people who need it, and it is really important that we flip this, and I often talk about this, reframing things, and reframing how you are looking at things, so there is a meme that you have probably seen on Facebook, that talks about the early mornings, being grateful that I have children that wake me up, it's a mummy type of meme, for the mess, I've got a full heart, it's about reframing lots of things, 'What if nobody buys?' Well what if stacks of people buy? And what if by you sitting on this product or service you're actually not allowing those people to buy.

'What if I can't do this?'

Well CAN'T isn't a word that we like to use, my little girl has a little mantra that she used in reception class at school and their little mantra was 'I can if I try' and if you put everything into this, if it is aligned to you, if you sort out your mindset, then you can achieve the most amazing things, you know the door is open for you to achieve anything that you desire if you are ready to do it, IF you are aligned to the mission, IF the mission becomes bigger than the fear, and we will talk about that a bit more.

'What if I can't handle it if it does work?' I hear people talking about their fear of failure a lot, but actually so often lots of people fear success too and it always seems like one that is super uncomfortable for people because their initial reaction is 'no, no, no', 'I want to be success I'm am ready to be a success' but actually when you dive down into it and you look at it further you know they're worried about what that change will make the world they are worried about what that change for the people around them.

They may well catastrophize the fact that what *if this is successful then I'm not going to be able to have the life that I have right now I'm not going to be able to be private and personal, people might be mean to me* and so often you know it not being aligned to the success and fearing the success is as common as fearing the failure. The other one that's really common is that you will never make it, doesn't matter what you do you're never going to make this happen you can watch every masterclass in the world you can get involved with absolutely everything you could buy – every product, every program, you could coach with whoever you wanted but you're never going to make it, and that essentially is around confidence and is around mindset and so all of these come back to mindset. All of these beliefs come back to you.

Do You Ever Truly Have It Nailed?

I think that the truth is – it's never completely nailed. We all have days where were feeling a bit wobbly. We all have days where are some sort of self talk will appear, bite us on the butt AND do you know what? I work with lots of super successful business owners who still have times where they feel wobbly. I don't say this to make you heave your head into your hands and feel a stack of despair. It does get easier and you do gain much more control of it.

You need to know that whoever it is that you're looking up to, whoever is it you're seeing as an inspiration – chances are they don't truly have their shit together. None of us do if we are truly honest about it. There's times when we wing it, there's times when the self talk takes over and there's time where we feel stuck or wobbly.

Fear & Uncomfort

There might well be times in growing your business that fear becomes a companion. Let me set off here by saying – you don't have to be fearless in order to build a business. You DO need to know how to identify it and move beyond it.

Fear is its gripping and it's consuming. When fear rears it's ugly head you will feel really, really stuck, you'll feel like you've just stopped you'll feel like there's mud up to your knees and there is absolutely no way for you to trudge through it.

Don't get fear confused that feeling that's attached to growth – that feeling of uncomfort. They are separate beasties.

I find that fear is gripping and you can FEEL it whereas uncomfort often manifests itself more in the head, it's more critical and more general unease. Unease that you're doing stuff you've never done before or moving in directions that you've never moved in before.

There will be times in your business where you will feel fearful. I see so often those motivational quotes doing the rounds that say that you have to fearless to build a business and quite frankly that's BS.

You need to learn to feel that fear, allow it to wash over you and act regardless of how you might feel on the inside.

When you step beyond your fear then your comfort zone actively sprints after you in an attempt to catch you up. Therefore moving your comfort zone forwards with every step you take.

Uncomfortable as a separate little beastie is exactly the same as those jeans, you know the ones, they become a little snug and start to feel uncomfortable – it purely a sign that you have grown, and that you are going through a growth stage It's the same in business, there will be times where you feel uncomfortable, there will be times where you've stepped outside your comfort zone, don't confuse fear with uncomfort.

Fear is that one that completely washes over you, overwhelms you and keeps you in one place, feeling uncomfortable is the one that's a little more clenched and feelings of 'Jeez!!! what is going to happen, I'm going to press it I'm going to press send..........go' and then that sicky feeling.

Being more mindful of how you feel is important. Whatever feelings are coming up it's important that you feel them. Feel those feelings and let them wash over you. Stop and have a little pity party if you need to but know that you're not going to stay there. If you try to kid yourself into believing you don't feel these feelings then actually you will stay in that vibration and feeling for MUCH longer.

Over-thinking

I bet you've been there before – you are questioning every single move. It's that time where you simply can't avoid asking questions. You've gone through every possible outcomes, you are questioning actually which way do you need turn AND REALLY what actually do you need to be doing?

An easy trap to fall into – over-thinking will keep you stuck because you feel indecisive and at times have totally catastrophized EVERYTHING.

My advice? I will always say go back to simplicity. Simple but significant is the mantra here. You absolutely can build a big business by always taking the path of least resistance and looking at what is the easiest and quickest solution to whatever is coming up for you at that moment. Taking the simple route means that you will start moving forwards and therefore will stop over-thinking. Movement is movement and starting to move forwards will allow you to gain momentum. We so often look for this complex, convoluted way of dealing with things – always draw it back to the obvious and simple solutions.

Procrastination

Hey lovely, another one that can keep you stuck. Procrastination means that you lack clarity and you find it ridiculously difficult to make decisions, in fact you avoid making decisions and therefore you are avoiding taking action,

The two most important things you need to do in your business are

- Making decisions
- Taking action

One thing I do want to tell you, that might just set you free here, is – by saying yes to one direction, one product, one path forwards YOU ARE NOT saying no to other things. You're simply saying "not right now." You're not neglecting or rejecting other possibilities. You're just going to focus your attention in one way for the time being.

Back to procrastination, so when you are stuck in procrastination you're not making decisions and you're not taking any action.

You're stuck inside your head.

I'd start by writing out your options and choices. I find that you have a whole stack more clarity when things are written down. There's power in the pen.

You can start to look at which direction or decision you are going to focus your attention on.

It's important to know that when you chose NOT to decide you make a decision to stay stuck. When you chose not to decide you make a decision to stay stuck. When you chose not to take action for the fear of taking the wrong action you chose to stay stuck.

So this is a choice.

Look at the simplest ways out of it and start to take action. Action will result in momentum and momentum will yield results.

Comparison

Comparison, oh my word, this one is such a common one and can absolutely keep you super stuck. I've got to say that I've fallen for this bad boy before and I know, for a fact, that the majority of entrepreneurs do at some time or another. Why do we do it? We do it because we naturally want to keep an eye on the people who might well be on our clients radar. We also want to consider where we feel we are in the hierarchy of life & business. It's feels really uncomfortable to see that written down but I suppose there's a little bit of a pack mentality about it.

Is there really any competition?

Here's the facts;

there are other people marketing to your crowd,

there are other people doing similar things to what you are doing,

But hang on – the whole concept of competition is it's you vs them

Whereas, the reality is that if you are building relationships with people then it isn't you vs them.

I think that this one is one we often witness in children as they grow up. They feel like they have to bustle for their positioning in life. We feel a little sad to see it and our advice to our kids is that it's important that they are themselves and that it doesn't matter what other people think of them. YET, when we get stuck in comparison we are doing similar things to ourselves.

Comparison keeps us stuck because you end up feeling in a bit "meh." You go out there and look at what other people are doing. You fall into the whole self-comparison thing. The self talk fairy then chirps in with lots of "helpful" feedback around why you aren't as good as that person or why you haven't got your shit together like that person. It becomes an obsessive thought process but it's also super heavy. The emotion attached to self comparison makes you feel burdened and it's absolutely exhausting. The funny thing is it's totally unnecessary.

As you start to make your way in business you look at the marketplace, your starting to look at the things other people are doing. It can be inspirational (be careful, that inspiration doesn't overstep the mark and fall into the copying mode).

The important thing is, is that as you start to develop your business you need to bring that attention internally. If you are spending all of your time looking at what everyone else is saying or doing you are being distracted from the job at hand. You are investing time, effort, energy and attention into their business rather than into your own business.

You need to start to look at developing relationships with your crowd, in your way. It's time to start to focus on & truly believe people will buy from you because they want to buy from you. You need to focus your attention on talking to your audience in your way and cultivating relationship with them. Building those relationship is key. Every single day I ask myself "what can I do to serve the pants off my crowd today." This allows me to really focus on the stuff that's important and not only has that set me free but I know that it's been a game changer for lots of my gorgeous Rockstars too. When you do this you don't need to think about other competition, you don't need to think about the other things that are going on. It's you placing your eyes and attention in the right place.

We need to make sure that we are looking after the one thing we have got control over and that is us and our business. We don't have control over what other people are doing.

It we look at it from a really honest perspective too – looking on may well give us clues about what people are and aren't doing BUT it'll never ever tell a full story.

- If you get caught up with the competition, it can impact on friends and family relationships (your self esteem and self worth becomes wobbly),
- it can impact on your list building, website, your sales pages, selling, customer relationship and customer expectations, the way you serve and show up on a day to day basis.
- It can affect bad days it can effect pushing and hustling.
- It can mean you end up working too hard and you end up working long hours.
- It can affect you in a way that will result in you getting lost and often staying .
- It can mean that you are feeling that you need to fake it up a
- It will mean that on occasions you fall into judging and deciding what other people's intentions and motives are, and that isn't always cool.

Rather than self comparison, which I reckon I shelved (in the most part) quite a while ago now, I AM self critical.

The Rules Of Being Self Critical

I am my own biggest critic! No-one can be more critical of me than me!

Is that a bad thing?

Well I suppose it depends and I suppose the biggest factor is that whether your critical eye over what you do is purely focusing on the negatives and getting stuck in destructive thought patterns as a result.

Being critical isn't a BAD thing. I feel that it's been a major contributor to my business growth. I am always prepared to take a look at the good, the fabulous, the bad and the ugly and take the learning points from what I have been doing and the results that has allowed me to achieve. It allows me to constantly evolve and grow and I never stagnate because I'm always looking at ways forward.

So, I'm talking about critical from the analysing sense of the word and not the picking apart and making yourself cry sense of the word BUT that's also super relevant in this conversation too...

WE ARE MUCH MORE CRITICAL OF OURSELVES THAN ANYONE ELSE WOULD EVER BE

So, I changed the banner picture on my Facebook Page a little while ago – my beautiful graphic designer (Vicki Nicolson – Brand Creative) send me the first one through and I loved the concept but said – eeehhhh we can't use that photo, I look so jowly in that one! Too much chinage!

Now, you're going to see it immediately as I've pointed it out to you BUT she said that she saw a picture that was full of energy, warm and enigmatic, that it was on brand and lovely. She was right, I wasn't. She saw what other people saw but all I saw was the chinage!

Yes I loved the concept and yes I look so jowly, look at that chinnage, we did change the photograph but kept the concept WHY I wouldn't have comfortably.... the one you see came from the concept BUT I wouldn't have comfortably and confidently worked on my Facebook page if I saw all those chins!

VAIN – yes! Lessons? Other people don't see what you see when it comes to you & your stuff – they don't see the imperfections (and don't get me wrong I'm perfectly happy with my imperfections and comfortable totally with who I am). I decided to go with a picture I liked better because it would mean I could keep my energy high on my page. Did it loose me any time – NO. Did it keep me stuck – NO. It's important that when you are over-thinking stuff (like the pictures of you, the stills you use on video posts, your website etc etc etc) that you think about whether you seeking your perfection (or dealing with a little vanity) is going to stop you from serving your crowd. Other people aren't going to see what you see. I'm here to show up, just as I am, but if I can have less chin-age then that's cool too!

73

The Moral Of This?

- Being critical is good for business ✓
- Looking at ways you can improve and evolve is good for business ✓
- Vanity may sneak in and it's your role to recognise it and decide whether it gets a place at the table. I'm not saying ignore it because if you ain't comfortable with something then you will NEVER EVER give it your best when it comes to marketing it or driving traffic to it and you'll always kinda wanna hide it. ✓
- You will see what others don't ✓
- Put your critical eye over things (do it subjectively and objectively where you can) BUT don't get stuck in negativity, get an outside opinion as it might simply be that you are too close ✓

Helpful Input From Others

Often people mean really well.

Often that's totally lost on us.

Let's talk about Helpful input from friends and family. Oh, don't you love it!

I know that this is such a common one that can absolutely knock you for six.

They might suggest that things aren't quite working out as you'd expected and you should perhaps consider going to find a "proper" job. They might make little comments about the fact that we should be millionaires by now with all the time and effort you're putting into your business. There might be stresses and strains around money.

I get it, when you're first starting out or you are looking to gain additional traction then it's super difficult to when other people don't "get" it or they can't quite see your vision for how things are going to develop.

It's important that you start to protect yourself the impact that this input has on you.

It's often not meant in any malice and it's not meant to be detrimental or negative. Often it's more about what you made it mean. I find that often this external input is brought to you from the most incredibly loving place and it's about people who love you seeking to protect you. Sometimes they may even feel that it's allowing you to have a "get out" if you want one.

If, right now, that kinda imput is making your wobbly then it's time to stop!

It can start to make you feel like you have to justify every action, that you are not doing things right,

Start off with the knowledge that, chances are, they mean well, they are looking out for your best interests,

It's time to take it with a pinch of salt.

So, I often smile politely, thank them for their comments and input and then just move on, every now and then my husband will have a time where he is going to tell me a little bit about what I could be or should be doing, sometimes there is little bits of food for thought in there, but other times, not so much so. It's about filtering what you want/need to hear and keeping the door to communication open.

Stop making it mean a shed load of other things with the inferences you've drawn yourself.

Discuss how it's unhelpful or makes you feel wobbly.

Drop it in the "fuck it" bucket.

Crack on with your plans and strategy because, the funny thing is, once you start to see results then the input that makes you wobbly diminishes and it's impact upon you ceases – you then have evidence that it's not true and wobbles/self talk cannot exist alongside evidence to the contrary.

why running your own business is like being pregnant

UNSOLICITED ADVICE!!

I remember being pregnant and everyone who met you had a little nugget of advice to give you – some were wonderful golden nuggets and some a crock of crap.

The tactic I used was to not let any of it get under my skin. The "helpful" stories about labour nightmares, the "MUST" be/do/have from the realms of the parenting world and the whole "you can't ignore this" stuff that would bombard me & my bump.

I decided to filter it all, listen BUT definitely filter. As I say – some bits were helpful and some bits not so much so.

It's the same in business. People will want to offer you advice. It might be well meaning friends and family. It might be complete strangers at networking meetings and it might be people that are urged to contact you in order to tell you what you can do better. Aaaaahhhhhh (sigh)

I'm not naive and there is sometimes a nugget or two in there. I have written a blog in the past about helpful tips I have received from the most unlikely of sources BUT please do filter it, please don't let it get under your skin or take it personally. Most people do mean well and feel that they are doing you a favour. Thank them, smile and decide which gets filed in the "heap of crap" drawer and which might just have some legs.

Boundaries

It's so important that you put boundaries in place within your business as soon as possible. If you are working every hour in the world that's not good for business. If you are constantly attached to work, head in your phone or your computer then that's not good for relationships.

If you are constantly working and not switching off then you have no boundaries.

If you are answering client queries at 10pm on a Saturday evening then you have no boundaries.

You make a rod for your own back. You create a beast. You then create an expectation that you will do this all the time.

You are a business owner and whilst serving your crowd and being reactive is AWESOME it's not to be done at a price.

You need to put professional and personal boundaries in place. Set expectations and yes, by all means, go ahead and exceed those expectations BUT don't do it at the cost of your own health and well-being.

77

A Quick Word On Burnout

You aren't building this business at a l costs.

You need to avoid burnout like the plague. Burnout sucks. You need to respect yourself and treat yourself like a leader. You need to plan in periods of rest, periods when you aren't selling and don't need to sell, periods of downtime.

These rest periods allow you to stop, re-group and move up to the next level.

Harness Your Mojo.

When you're in the zone then crack on. Harness your creativity and write when you are in the mood to write. Record videos or audios when you are in the mood to record.

If you're not in the zone then please step away. If you're not in the zone you will just end up creating rubbish stuff and get REALLY annoyed and frustrated.

Elizabeth Gilbert in her awesome book Big Magic (if you haven't read it then this one's definitely on the recommended list) talks about having an affair with your creativity. Think of it as stolen time, time that you will protect fiercely, the time that you will take and grasp whenever it makes itself available. It's love and passion and a giddy feeling in your stomach. **Remember...**

> 66
>
> "We can't always control out circumstances, but we can always control out attitude towards our circumstances."
>
> *Rebecca Fox*

Integrity

Your integrity must be one of your most fiercely protected assets. Once lost it's very difficult to regain.

Your integrity is about you being true. You don't want to be telling people porky pies and making them have reasons not to trust you.

When your integrity is called into question it cuts like a knife. It's the most difficult one in the world to swallow.

How could they question me in that way? Your integrity may well be called into question (regardless of how fiercely you protect it) but you have the confidence and ability to know that you are being true and honest in everything that you do.

A Rockstar doesn't tell untruths and does everything from a place of giving and serving. This is how your fans will perceive you. Others may have views but remember that they don't know you. There will always be people out there who are quick to question you.

This is usually their stuff and NOTHING to do with you.

One last one. I touched on this one earlier but it's definitely worth a repeat! My little girl was busy watching Cinderella the other day. She's a sensitive little soul when it comes to the movies but there's a little mantra I have taught her that applies in life (& the majority of children's movies!). "If it ain't happy then it's not the end" (BUT please what is it with Disney films and the amount of parental deaths).

79

Are You A Princess?

There is ONE THING that we all do and it comes REALLY naturally to most of us – that OVERCOMPLICATING the heck out of EVERYTHING!!

I am sure you have been there - you are staring at your computer screen, you are sure it must be possible but you have no idea how to make it work. You are stuck. Eeeekkk – it's pants, you just feel worn out with thinking abou⁻ how exactly you are going to make this happen.

Now, I am a glass half full kinda girl and I will often be heard spouting about being solutions based and not problems. For every problem there is a solution. ⁻or every worn out woman looking at a computer screen there is often a very, very simple answer. Sometimes, though, we just can't see it. We are too close and for the life of us we can't see it.

So what do we do?

That's right...

We try to make it even more complicated. We take that problem and we end up magnifying it into an epic, convoluted system of a million different tasks to get the result we desire.

We make it a mammoth task.

Guess what, often the answer is uber duber super easy.

I have been in this place. I have been there sat in front of a piece of software. I am clear on the outcome I desire, just no idea on how to get there.

I am getting frustrated. I am the solutions lady not the problem lady.

How can I be in this tearing my hair out place?

- Do I step back to look at the bigger picture? NO I DON'T!

- Do I take my own advice & look for the easy solution? NO I DON'T!

- Do I stop, just for a moment and take stock? OF COURSE NOT!

- Do I outsource it and ask for help? NO, I GOT IT COVERED, OBVIOUSLY! (sense the sarcasm and desperation creeping in)

I sit there and I get increasingly frustrated. This should be a 30 minute job, max! Oh my word, what's wrong with me? Have I had a complete mental block? Why am I making this so difficult?

So, I send a support request to the help desk.

The reply I got, from a lady called Princess, made me face palm!

Oh my word, how had I missed that simple solution, why had I overlooked simple in exchange for the convoluted solutions I had been trying.

Now, I don't remember the names of all the people who have ever helped me via support desks but this lady stuck with me. Why? Because I now have a Princess Principle.

Whenever I think I might be overcomplicating things I run the Princess Principle filter. I step back and I overview the problem and look for the obvious, simple solutions.

The Princess Principle

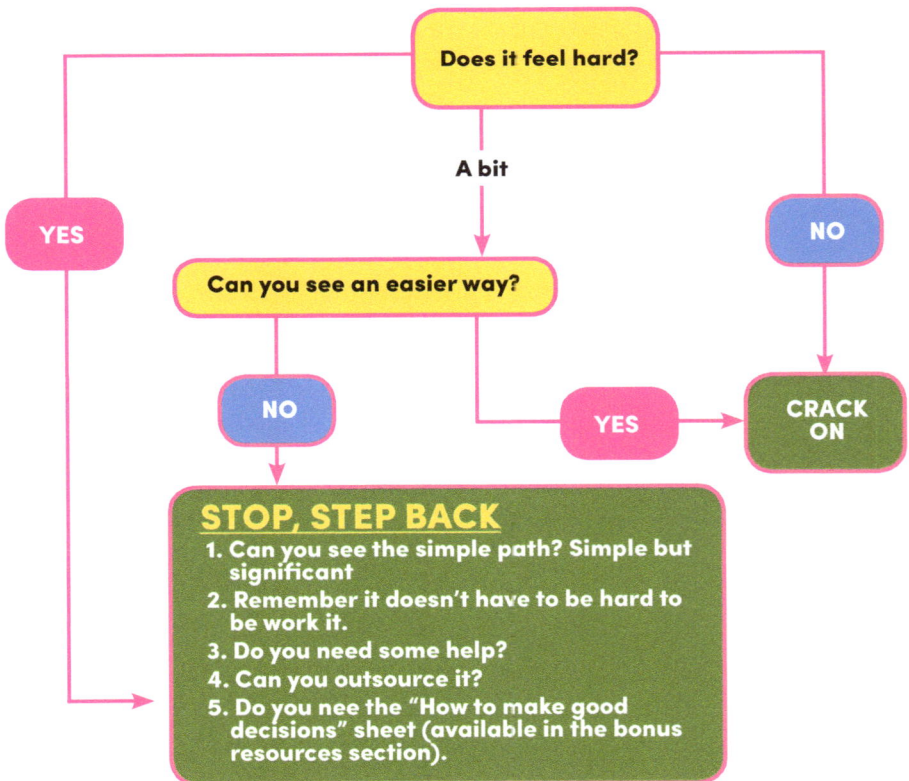

```
                    ┌──────────────────┐
                    │  Does it feel hard? │
                    └──────────────────┘
                              │
                            A bit
                              │
        YES                   ▼                    NO
                    ┌──────────────────┐
                    │ Can you see an easier way? │
                    └──────────────────┘
                         │
                        NO                YES ──→  CRACK
                         │                          ON
                         ▼
          ┌──────────────────────────────────────┐
          │ STOP, STEP BACK                        │
          │ 1. Can you see the simple path? Simple but │
          │    significant                          │
          │ 2. Remember it doesn't have to be hard to │
          │    be work it.                          │
          │ 3. Do you need some help?               │
          │ 4. Can you outsource it?                │
          │ 5. Do you nee the "How to make good     │
          │    decisions" sheet (available in the bonus │
          │    resources section).                  │
          └──────────────────────────────────────┘
```

As humans we are oh so inclined to try to make things difficult. It might be because we are brought up thinking that things are not meant to be easy. That anything worth doing is difficult and complicated, that we have to have a super duper techy solutions to all problems or that we are not as ept at a certain task as we would like to be. We get in our own way.

Never overcomplicate things in your business. There is no need. You are much better making your business as simple as possible and flow with ease than end up overcomplicating things and making it difficult. My mantra is SIMPLE BUT SIGNIFICANT.

Often we end up in positions where things are overcomplicated because that's how we have always done things. It doesn't need to be that way. Call yourself on things that you are complicating.

The lesson – things don't need to be hard, things don't need to be difficult, just apply the Princess Principle!

Some Pointers & Checklist

So, some easy ways to keep a check on mindset, lets get some practical ways of helping you:

- Write stuff down, if journaling is a big commitment or something you don't do or something that is a bit airy fairy, then lets not talk about it as journaling, simply just write stuff down, anything that is keeping you stuck, write it down, discharge it of any power it has, discharge it of any energy it has, decide it if is a truth or lie, you can keep that notebook, you can keep that scrap of paper, you can keep that journal and see if there are any patterns forming, things to work on. Or if you feel you don't want anyone else to see it you can burn it, I have to say in a safe way because my husband works for the fire services, so if you are going to burn it please burn it as a responsible adult in a safe a way and move on.

- Disassociate yourself with the attachment of the outcome, it doesn't matter what the outcome is, simply align to your mission, get on and serve, the chances are the rest of it will fall into place.

- Avoid the drama, some people relish it, keep away from it, take a big old deep detour away from that

- Check ins, get an accountability partner, get somebody who gets what you are trying to achieve, who gets the journey, who gets what it is like to be self-employed, who gets to be in this position, it might be this is somebody who you know, it might be somebody who is a coach or a mentor, whoever it is get some accountability, get to help one and other. Surround yourself with positivity.

- Cheerleaders – really important, surround yourself with cheerleaders, who want the best outcome for you, who are there to support you when you need it, anchor in the positivity, I do face to face events, I do 1:1 work and so often people go away and they are ready, they are absolutely ready, it might be that after reading this you feel absolutely ready, what I suggest is you anchor that feeling as soon as you can, and some people talk about anchoring it into a part of your body, for me I anchor it into music so I can put that song on and return to that place of total motivation, so I will sit and listen to that song when I am absolutely top of the world, when I am feeling on it, and I will think about how I am feeling in that moment, I will anchor those feelings into that piece of music so whenever I am wobbling I can go back to that piece of music and I can use it over and over again to get me back into that place.

- Real life strategies for showing up when you feel a bit wobbly, take some time to review your social media, go to about sections make sure you have a picture of you on your profile picture, showing up can be really small easy steps, use videos and Facebook lives on social media, if it scares the pants of you now, it's time to flood yourself and practise, like I said sometimes when we do flood technique I send people off to do 10 videos, sometimes its about getting it out of your own way and the mission is greater than the fear.

- Use pictures of yourself in your social media, let me connect with you, don't be the same old same old, check in with your website about me page, look at social media, I work on the basis that I need to be around about every 10 posts on social media. What is massively important when you are looking at building your business and mindset, look at ways you can serve and support your crowd, look at things you can do to make the world a better place, look at things you could do to help people on their journey for free, the things you can help them with in exchange for an email address and the things you can do in a product and a programme, which they will purchase, because this is all about helping people, whether it is a physical product that helps people feel better about themselves, whether it is a physical product to help them to get to somewhere else in their world, whether it is a physical produc- that makes them feel good, or whether it is a service that you provide to help and support them, think of the ways you can do that.

- Stop pretending and show up in your own glorious space – YOU DO NOT NEED TO BE ANYONE ELSE, you do not need to speak like other people or write in a way that other people write, you don't need to give yourself rules, and STOP please please please for the love of everything STOP beating yourself up, and giving yourself this unachievable standard to get to, you don't need to give yourself rules. You've got permission to be yourself 100% yourself, no filters although brush your hair, out of your yoga pants and take of your slippers now and then because that will make you feel better too.

- People buy from people, people are out there right now that need what you have to offer, let them get to know you, like you and trust you, then they will invest in you, you need to be the perfect solution to their problem and you need to be the right person to help them on that journey, when that mission is bigger than the fear, then glorious glorious things will happen.

The calculation for Thinking Like a Rockstar:
Your Boundaries + Protecting Those Boundaries + Your Creativity + What You Want + You Being A Leader + Integrity + not overcomplicating stuff = Thinking Like A Rockstar

CHAPTER REMINDER CHECKLIST

Remember...

Think about your bigger picture – what do you really want in your business?

Embrace creativity when it strikes and leave it when it feels forced.

Protect your integrity at all costs.

The Princess Principle – is it really that complicated?

7 MARKET
LIKE A ROCKSTAR

Let's get some things out of the way first.

Marketing is a long-term relationship and not a one night stand.

Social media is NOT a popularity contest. It's not about who has the most likes, followers or fans. These numbers are mere vanity. It's a place for you to connect with your fans. It's a place for you to cultivate, nurture and build relationships. It's a social platform for (you guessed it) being SOCIAL!!

You want your fans to engage with you, to be on your email list, to seek advice from you, to indulge in your website and read your blogs. You want them to work with you and buy your products.

You want to serve them and you want them to find you useful and relevant. You want to help them change their world. You want to attract more of them into your crowd.

It's all about you and them but not in the traditional THEM & US kinda way. These are the two points you need to get right and be able to communicate within your marketing.

It's about letting you shine and you serving them.

This is what your marketing is all about. Marketing is about much more than your advertising and seeking customers. Marketing is everything that you do, public facing, within your business. If the word "marketing" makes you feel uneasy then my suggestion to you is that the simply swap the word. Marketing is about communicating so instead of being stuck on the word marketing, simply swap it for communication & connection.

Marketing is about:

- Introducing new people to you & your business
- Building relationships
- Nurturing relationships
- Helping people
- Your brand awareness
- Your brand image
- Your image
- Your content
- Staying top of mind
- Staying in touch
- Building your list
- Letting people get to know you, like you and trust you.
- Offering people opportunities to work with you.
- It manifests itself through your communications whether they are images, writing, audio or videos.

It brings together your online and offline presence.

You will have a marketing mix that brings together lots of different elements. This isn't something that will happen in the blink of an eye and marketing certainly ain't no one trick pony.

You will cultivate your marketing strategy and your marketing mix. At the moment you will not see lots of the mix as marketing. You will probably see it as just things that you do.

You might just be going through the motions.

The other thing to know is that marketing isn't a task you can ever tick off your to do list and just when you think you've got your head around it all the rules change.

Now let me tell you what's really easy...

What is really easy is to vomit stuff out there. I know that lots of my lovely clients start off doing this. There is a sense of urgency. Almost a panic. They need to get something out there, anything. The quality of what they do ends up being compromised as they just spew more and more stuff "out there".

Their videos are done on a wing and a prayer.

They are either knocking out blogs willy nilly with no strategy or thought behind them or they are procrastinating for days about how they can write the next blog. Their images aren't thought through.

Quick get something out there, anything, fill the silence – NOW!!!

There is a lack of forethought. It's not their fault and it's definitely not a criticism. It's normal.

It feels a little bit like a chase. Let's just get some information out there – just anything, quick, I need to have a presence.

91

My Marketing Beginnings

I would rather you had a thoughtful presence than a vomited presence. Thoughtful is much nicer than vomit! I want you to know something – less is more (if more is shite). There's no perfect formula to this BUT know that putting nothing out there is better than putting shit out there. Marketing was something I started doing in the corporate world. I had no formal marketing training but I knew, even from the very outset, that it was all about building relationships. It was all about people knowing that you were the BEST solution to their problem.

I was a family lawyer (there is much more about me & my journey at the back of the book if you're interested) and I knew that the product that I offered was essentially a distress product. It wasn't something people bought into just because! It was very rare that someone wanted to be instructing a lawyer and throwing money at legal fees. It wasn't something people wanted to spend their money on. They were at their lowest ebb when they consulted with me initially. Their world was falling apart. They were going to tell me things that they never spoke about even to their nearest and dearest.

I would sit in marketing meetings and the marketing team would pop across buzz words like "brand awareness" and "thinking outside the box" <<<< ack!!!!! If you've ever seen those marketing/corporate speak spoof bingo boards you will know what I mean and I can say that I would have always been calling "house" during those marketing meetings.

MY SECTOR MARKETING BOLLOCK BINGO

#1 secret	Work Less (3-6 secs per week) & earn more (a gazillion dollars	Ahead of the trends	ROI
Ducks in a row	Passive Income	Squeeze Page	Traffic Warm/Cold
Hot leads	I've got all my shit together	Overnight success	Viral
Challenge	Swipe File	Steal My Scripts	Takeaways

I would plant seeds of ideas for marketing campaigns that we could do but I would keep being drawn back to the fact that people would need to know, like and trust me in order to share their deepest, darkest secrets with me.

It's funny to see that when we have fast forwarded a few years, some of my marketing campaigns have now been used in the legal practices I worked in. On a plus side (and as a demonstration of how relationships were important to me) I got some golf lessons out of my marketing budget in order to spend time with prospective clients and sources of referral. I don't play golf now but, as I tell my kids, you should always try new things.

Anyhaps, back to the overarching corporate marketing strategy...

I decided that I would work on relationship building as my marketing in the corporate world. I would network with other professionals who would refer work to me. I wouldn't be stuffy and unapproachable. My work demanded that people got to know a bit of me. I would spend time with the ladies who ran the Women's Refuge – not only did this work light me up, it was my reason for choosing law, but it also meant that I got the work referrals.

When I left the corporate world I thought that I had a reasonable grounding in marketing. I think that I was misleading myself a little here. I had MUCH more to learn and learn I did. I set about soaking up all the information that I could.

I am still a firm believer in the fact that your marketing starts (and finishes) with the know, like and trust factor. When people are investing in YOU helping them then you cannot be aloof and distant but at the same time you can't be readily available and on tap (otherwise there will be no point in your fans paying for your products as they have access to you in any event).

I also learnt that my know, like and trust needed to be coupled with my who, what & why.

Who Are You Talking To?

It's all well and good to let people get to know me, like me and trust me but who were these people, what was the problem I could fix for them and why should they even care?

Traditionally lots of people talk about this as an Ideal Client Avatar. This kept me REALLY stuck when I attempted to craft a profile of the perfect person – I felt like I needed to include a shoe size and the colour of their underwear.

I crafted a totally different approach.

Why?

Because it's still super important to know who you are talking to because this will set you free in terms of your marketing strategy and message. BUT I decided that commonality was much better than specificity in this case.

You can get your hands on how I do this exercise in the resources available with this book – www.beabusinessrockstar.com

These are the fans I've been talking about.

To work out who you are talking to I suggest that you start by asking yourself these questions:-

The Existing Biz Questions – if you already have clients

- Who do you love working with?
- Why do you love working with them?
- Who makes your heart sing?
- What do they have in common? This one might bring about some massive revelations. I know it did for me the first time I did it!
- Now it's time for you to move on to the new biz questions too.

New Biz Questions

- Who would you love to work with?
- Who (right now) do you think you could bring the biggest change and results to?
- Who can you help get unstuck?
- What is it in their life that's making them miserable?
- What keeps them awake at night/makes them wake up in the early hours of the morning?
- Look at drafting their Rockstar Journey – where is their stucksville and where is their place of awesome? What challenges might they meet along the way? Where could they get stuck? Where might they panic or go into fear?
- What are they saying to themselves? Try to tune into their self talk and see what you can find out.

Ok so before you hurtle off there's one last thing that I need to address here THEY NEED TO VALUE WHAT YOU DO AND AFFORD TO PAY FOR IT!

I have spent some time looking at people who fall into the trap of getting their brains picked. I have fallen into that trap myself in the past too. These people rarely become paying clients and these people (more often than not) don't value you.

There is a Raving Fans Workbook available in the bonus resources that accompany this book, access it here >>> www.beabusinessrockstar.com

Placing Your Attention In The Right Places

It's important that your marketing attention is focused in the right places. You can't be EVERYWHERE all of the time. You need to make some decisions.

- Where is your marketing time and budget best spent?
- Where are your fans most likely to hang out?
- What can you do to make sure that your marketing does not eat up every hour of your day and every day of your week?

The next layer that comes into play within your marketing is the different levels of relationship you have with your fans. You need to work on strategies to attract those who you haven't met yet, nurture relationships with those who have been in some form of contact with you and then develop those fans into clients and clients into repeat clients.

It can sound confusing but essentially:

Those You Haven't Met Yet (known as cold traffic) = how are you going to attract new fans into your business?

Nurturing Relationships With Those Who Have Had Content With You (known as warm traffic) = adding value, getting, showing them a bit of who you are and what you're all about and bringing them further into your work i.e. getting them to sign up for your list or become active on your Social Media etc. Engaging them I suppose, we are kinda dating and hanging out here but don't be the knobber who just disappears after we've had a nice time.

Develop Fans Into Customers (known as hot leads) = make sure that you are offering your fans the solution to their problems and making sure that that solution is the right solution.

Turning Your Buyers Into Repeat Buyers = this one is a little more tricky, as I believe that you need to handle this one with care. I don't see my customers as walking purses and I am not an advocate of extracting every last penny out of each of my purchasers in order to get the maximum client return value. Does this cost me money – yes it probably does BUT I make sure I respect my clients. BUT that coesn't mean I don't offer my clients other products. I look at other ways I can help them to achieve their goals and keep their businesses moving forwards.

Everything You Produce

Everything that you produce in your business is content. So let's talk about content. It comes from one idea. It might be that you are inspired to write a blog or create a video or an audio.

When you first start out it's all very ad hoc, it's reactionary. The idea washes over you like a wave and you grab your surf board and jump onto it.

That's fine BUT...

I want you to know that most people are only allowing their content to have a microscopic element of its potential! Yes, really! They are kinda letting their content down but we'll talk a little more about that soon.

⭐ It's Rockstar Challenge Time Again...

I have a little challenge for you. I want you to write down a list of your specialist subjects. Everything that you teach your clients. I want you to write this list without filter. I want an unedited list of all the things you could talk about within your business.

Everything.

Then you can apply a little filter – **Just Because You Could Doesn't Mean You Should.** This is a little mantra I use with my clients regularly.

Let's talk about that.

Ok, so I could teach all sorts of weird and wonderful things. I could teach you how to build a website but to be honest it's totally not my thing. I can do it, I have learned stacks about web design, coding and bringing together basic sites but do you know what – it doesn't light a fire in my heart.

Just because I could doesn't mean I should.

99

I could teach you how to get techie and set up a membership site and again, yes, it's part of a bigger programme but solo it just doesn't work.

Just because I could doesn't mean I should.

I tested this concept in My Project 100k and the answer remained the same. I tried putting out products on a just because I could basis and this didn't do anything for my income, your brand or my enthusiasm.

You can look at the areas you have written down, cross off the areas that you don't think match with your fans. Everything else can stay for now. I'm not going to let you run off and make products to sell out of them all but they are a good little resource for you to have and refer back to.

If you are ever stuck wondering what this week's blog could be about then you can refer back there and re-connect with your specialist subjects. Add these subjects into your crowd notebook for safe keeping too.

The topics you have written down form your Mastermind specialist subject and these are topics you will cover in order to help your fans.

You will create content from these topics.

Wheel Ain't For Re-inventing

Now, a little revelation for you >> you don't have to reinvent the wheel.

This is where we arrive back at the fact that we only ever allow our content a microscopic element of its whole potential.

We painstakingly prepare it.

We put it out there on our Facebook page, perhaps, and that's it – it's done!

Oh my, oh my! Don't we make things difficult for ourselves at times?

Lots of the content you create will have multiple purposes. That blog you write, that can go on your website, be the main article in your newsletter, you can share it on Facebook, Twitter, Pinterest, LinkedIn. You can take quotes from it to use on social media too. You can also record a video about the same topic and pop it on YouTube plus, again, share it on social media, you can take the video and rip out the audio from it in order to produce a podcast. When you created the blog you will probably do an image to accompany the blog, well you can use that image on Pinterest, Instagram and other social media platforms.

Not only can you spread the piece of content across multiple platforms but you can also make it into multiple medias. That blog you wrote could become a video or a podcast or a Facebook post. That video you recorded can become a blog or a podcast. Your content and subjects can be written, visual, recorded or audio – now that's a LOT of potential in each piece of content.

Your content can be used in so many different ways.

You don't have to create different content for every one of your different platforms.

Think about how many ways you can use everything.

Also, this content should not only ever get out for an airing once. Recycling is good (haven't you heard?) Re-use old stuff.

Not everyone sees everything you put out there.

Sorry!!! I know you know this but I also know that your ego tells you that people will feel like you are short changing them if you share the same thing again. This isn't the truth!!

Re-use and recycle.

Re-work and re-publish.

You do need to make a choice about the platforms that will get your attention as you don't have time to focus on them all.

For me, my attention is place on my website, my list/e-marketing Facebook, You Tube, podcasting and Instagram and I run my other platforms more passively (and share the content from my predominant focus places).

Where do you need to be?

Where are your fans most likely to find you?

Your website (a no-brainer for everyone, as if you apply a little SEO then the search engines should be able to find you).

- Facebook (despite MASSIVE declines in organic reach Facebook is still an amazing platform to do business)
- Twitter (fast speed so use good hashtags). It's kinda like the outside lane of the motorway. Things move VERY fast, so don't be afraid to post more often
- YouTube (it's the second largest search engine in the world only behind Google – can you capitalise on this? If you are saying no then you are in trouble – tut tut)
- LinkedIn (where you'll find more professional/corporate clients)
- Pinterest (still a female dominated crowd)
- Instagram (great image platform and there's no reason why you can't use it even without a visual/product based business– don't get caught in the trap of thinking your business isn't a visual one).
- E-marketing (a MUST)
- Podcasting (tap into the iTunes audience)
- Events (get in front of real life people)
- Networking (meet and interact)

This list IS NOT designed for you to beat yourself around the head with (and is my no means exhaustive) and say there's so much I'm not doing, how will I ever cover it all, I'm completely overwhelmed by the options, how will I ever make an impact yada yada yada? Stop it already.

What you need to do is pick a few to place your attention.

Right, before you go wobbling off about closing the door to opportunity or get your knickers in a knot about only being in one place right now – STOP!!

I work on the basis of primary and secondary platforms.

These are not set in stone.

You can tweak and change your choices as you work out what works for you.   You just can't do it all at once.

So your Rockstar marketing is about much more than which platform it's about how you want to be seen & heard. It's about standing out in a busy, noisy world. It's about connecting with your fans and building that relationship.

The important things you need to think about are:

- Giving away a little bit of yourself
- Giving away a little bit of your knowledge
- Being consistent with your messages
- Sharing good quality stuff
- Adding Value
- Inspiring
- Teaching
- Entertaining
- Injection of your personality is a MUST too.

The one single factor that can help you connect with your crowd and build relationships is probably the one that scares you the most. It's probably the one that you have only dipped your toe into and will only do if you ABSOLUTELY HAVE TO.

The one thing is VIDEO.

Video has been king of content recently because video brings about a deeper level of connection. Video allows your crowd to put a face and a voice, mannerisms and connection to your brand.

Before you start that wobble about what you look like and what you sound like then stop it already.

You will overanalyse this much more than your fans do.

This is where you have to be brave.

What's the worst that can happen?

I spoke to one of my client's recently about it and said "would you care if I put on 6 stone but still helped you in the same way?" Her answer: "no, of course not". Point made. It doesn't matter what I look like or what I sound like. It matters how much I can help!

Ok, so let's look at some specifics in your marketing...

Website Rockstars

Let's start with your website. Your best brand presence is your website BUT what is your website really for?

Are you using your website as the shop window for the world?

It kinda goes without saying now that your website needs to be mobile compatible.

But, beyond that, what do you need?

You need to make sure that your website isn't a DIY schlop together, I'm not saying that you can't do it yourself and in the bonuses available with this book I've popped some good recommended programmes there for you to embrace your own web design. What I mean is that it can't be a whole homemade mess. If you are a Rockstar then your website needs to go pro too.

Over the years I have become super web savvy. I have built lots of little websites and done lots of work on my own website. But do you think that I would be putting my own "schlepped together" website out there now? Definitely NOT. My website is beautifully designed BUT more than that it's been very much thought through. My website hasn't been a place of kneejerk reactions.

Where did I start?

The first thing I started with was the Look and Feel of my site. I wanted my website to be OBVIOUSLY mine. I wanted it to have its own little heart beat and to ooze my personality. I wanted it to be captivating and interesting, I wanted it to look good but I also wanted it to have shedloads of content and be the most amazing resource for business owners. It needed to be easy to navigate and include the key content that I wanted there.

From my brand and concepts/colours came some new professional photographs. Again, you NEED to go pro here. Your hollibops snaps won't cut it, you need some fantastic, professional photographs doing that will reflect you and your personality. Think them through.

106

What are you like?

I made the mistake in the past of having a studio shoot, in a black dress, with a black necklace. I became black and white. I had become boring by virtue of my pictures (I showed you those piccies in the branding section). I'm not boring. I have a colourful personality.

Sometimes I even wear myself out.

So the image and **look** of your site is really important (and that includes how you portray you within there too). WHAT YOU ARE NOT TO DO is compare yourself to others now. Ack, I'm not skinny and blonde and in my twenties. Well, I'm not. I 'm a little rounder than I used to be, if I don't get my hair done I have silver glistens around my scalp and unfortunately (no balls to that – FORTUNATELY) my twenties are behind me.

I've heard it before. Aaaahhh, well, I could do this if I was 80lbs ringing wet and had big blonde hair >> if you feel like that then it's time to head back to Rockstar Confidence because you need to be comfortable being you. Being a Rockstar isn't all about being super duper airbrushed and massively polished, it's about being confidently and perfectly you and being the BEST version of you.

Next we will move onto the content on your website. Your website content needs to place you as an expert and it needs to be there to help and nurture your audience. Your content needs to be written from the soul, with you running all the way through it. You need to add and keep up to date with blogs on your website.

You need to make sure that you are happy that the content reflects you and what you do.

So, what's your website for and what do you need to brainstorm around?

- It's for your FANS – what do they want/expect to see on there?
- It's a shop window to your business - are you showing yourself off well or does it look a little amateur right now? Be honest.
- It's to allow you to form relationships and nurture those relationships – how's your "about me" page looking right now? Can people find out how to find out more?
- It's for list building – do you have some fab freebies on there?
- It's for driving sales – do you have anything that people can buy on there?
- Is it establishing you as an expert – does it have good quality content and any credibility logos that you have gathered along the way from that, there PR that we talked about earlier?
- Are you proud of it?

Social Media

It continues to be a fab place to hangout although (sound like an old lady here), it's not like the good old days!! Once upon a time, a very very long time ago (Ok so not that long ago at all) social media took the world by storm and businesses were quick to react to this. I remember days when your organic reach was stoking and you could post things and LOADS of people would see them. I remember the days when organic likes came to your business page and you felt like a people magnet.

But, alas, those days have gone, they are no more. Social media is a different place now, it's busy and noisy and bustly. It's a place where you can often feel like you are shouting down a deep dark hole.

Lots of coaches will tell you that they build there tribe of a zillion followers with no ad budget at all. I'd like to see them do that now. I'd love to see them use the nuggets of advice that they share about building a tribe and try to implement that in the current climate, particularly on Facebook (without leveraging their established page). That's NOT TO SAY it's impossible to gather your fans on Facebook (or other social media platforms) anymore, it just means that you need to think, behave and implement differently.

Before we go any further there are a few important things to note...
- Social Media is SOCIAL
- Social Media ISN'T about you spewing stuff out there just to fill a silence
- Social Media ISN'T a popularity contest
- Social Media NEEDN'T be a time drain
- Social Media IS fab for building relationships

Your social media presence is part of your overall strategy and when you are going pro with your social media presence as you establish yourself as a Rockstar, then you MUST make sure that you STOP just throwing things out there willy nilly – the answer is NEVER something is better than nothing.

Think quality.

Think about being of service to your fans.

There is a marketing mix that you need to consider and you need to think about including any of the following that you have into your marketing mix:

- Blog shares
- Memes (pictures with text on them)
- Behind the scenes information and insights
- Videos
- Podcast links
- Information posts
- Inspirational posts
- Quotes
- Humour
- Questions
- Themed Posts – like Facebook Friday and Throw Back Thursdays.

You can also share things from other people's pages that you think will resonate with your fans – but please do so ethically <<< video available to show you how in the bonuses accompanying this book, access it here >>> www.beabusinessrockstar.com

I am all for inspiring my audience and giving them that jolt along that they need, a rallying of the troops if you like BUT please don't fall into the trap of being all guff and fluff, all style and no substance, or all fur coat and nay knickers (as my mother would say – a very North of England phrase indeed). Style without substance isn't serving your audience.

- Tell stories
- Be interesting
- Entertain
- Include some looks behind the scenes
- Make sure you are always thinking of your crowd
- Don't just chuck stuff out there
- Ask questions, be inquisitive
- Try new things & then try them again (it sometimes takes a little while to get traction)
- Invest in paid advertising methods on social media

You need to know that you can't be AWESOME on all of your social media Platforms. You need to choose your primary and secondary platforms.

So, how do you make this decision? Firstly, where are your fans most likely to hang out? I suppose the saying goes – fish where the fish are! If you decide on a platform where your fans are unlikely to be then you are unlikely to attract the number of fans you could. Secondly, it has to be a platform you are comfortable with. If you hate the social media platform then that will show, your energy just won't be right, you'll hate hanging out there. Confession time – I Emma Holmes bloomin detest LinkedIn (there I said it)... An edited note included in the absolute final edit of this book is that over recent months I think I've removed this block by looking at Linkedin in a very different way.

Your primary platforms need to be places you love and where your fans love too.

> "It's not our job to tell our audience where we live.
> It's to grow communities where they live."
>
> *www.postplanner.co.uk*

I would say that you should concentrate your efforts on no more than 2 platforms.

Your secondary platforms are places where you have a presence and visibility BUT you aren't spending stacks of times there. It might be that you automate lots of the presence on your secondary platforms and only dedicate small amounts of time each day/week.

Remember, as always, don't over-think this decision. It's not set in stone. If you choose 2 platforms and they don't really work for you then you can change your focus platforms. What I would suggest though is that you give your choices a little time in order to work before you decide that they aren't working. Marketing efforts take time to gain traction and the fruits of your labour take time to translate into real results.

E-Marketing

E-marketing is one of my favourites in the marketing arsenal too!

E-marketing allows you to fall into your fans inboxes on your terms and allows you to provide EVEN MORE value to your fans.

Emails aren't going anywhere. I hear lots of people talk about e-marketing being dead but I certainly don't see any evidence of that. Social media evolves and changes. The social media platforms control who does and doesn't see your content and there is an increasing frustration from people that, Facebook in particularly, has seen a massive downturn of reach and the algorithms constantly change and are unpredictable.

> 66
> "Only 1-6% of your fans are seeing your organic posts in their Facebook Feed the other 94% are not."
> *Mari Smith*

E-marketing...
- Keeps you top of mind
- Allows you to add more value to your crowd by giving them more help & advice
- Allows you to nurture relationships
- Allows you to establish yourself as an expert
- Allows you to share more with your crowd

What makes a good e-newsletter? The answer: it depends on your crowd.

How often should I send it? Again, it depends on your crowd.

E-newsletters vary massively and it's a good idea to make sure you keep an eye on them regularly. Become an observer. Which newsletters in your inbox do you love to open? What is it about them that makes your heart sing? What can you learn from the emails in your inbox?

I get asked ALL the time about open rates for newsletters. This is something that you definitely need to track. When you first start out and have a smaller list then you are likely to have a higher open rate. The longer you are sending out newsletters and the bigger your list gets then the smaller the open rate becomes. The industry average for coaches is apparently around the 18% mark. My current open rate is usually between 35-48%.

A lot of your email open rate can be determined by the subject line. You need to make the subject line in your emails a MUST to click on.

Remember, people's email inboxes are getting increasingly busy. Again, you need to stand out.

Apparently you should also avoid the words:
- Help
- % Off
- Reminder
- Free
- Anything that's in CAPS
- !! (more than one exclamation mark)

You need to become a student to your email open rates and which emails get the best open rates from your crowd, what they included and what the headline was. Unsubscribes is one that can definitely get under your skin.

When you first start out with e-marketing, an unsubscribe can break your heart and your spirits. You can feel really dejected that someone has clicked that unsubscribe button and even worse if they have taken it a step further and marketed your email as SPAM (how could they? **sobs**).

When people start out with their mailing list and in business it's very personal. Every subscriber makes you feel warm & fluffy inside and every unsubscribe leaves you feeling desperately upset and like you've personally offended people. It's really normal to feel this way.

I was talking to one of my Rockstars recently and said "would you rather have them on your list and be clogging up their inbox with something they don't want to hear about, perhaps vexing them a little but all the same you plopping in there every week, or would you like to set them free with love & light. It's important to know that those people who unsubscribe aren't the right match for you. It's not personal, it's not a judgement on your value or worth, it's simply the natural growth of your business.

- You won't be for everyone.
- Some people will simply join your list in order to get your freebie and then will disappear (I've chuckled about this one in the past when people have signed up, got their freebie and then unsubscribed and not knowing that even more freebies were on the way to their email if they had only just waited a few moments).
- You will outgrow some people.
- Some people will decide that you are simply not for them.

115

- Some people will find themselves on your list with more than one email address.

It's not personal.

I'd rather you had a smaller list of people who were **"into"** you and wanted to hear more from you and would ultimately buy from you than a big list of disinterested people.

The size of your list is vanity & ego. The sanity of your list is just how much those there are interested in what you have to say and ultimately what you have for sale.

It's ok to feel that little pang of regret at the beginning but I guarantee you that this will desensitize quite quickly when you start to see that this is totally normal and that it's the natural ebb and flow of your mailing list.

Now, let's address the other one....

OH MY WORD!! SOMEONE MARKED MY EMAIL AS SPAM!! HOW COULD THEY?!?!

It happens.

I have had people mark my email as SPAM who have been people who are in similar businesses to me (narky perhaps) and people who I know BUT do you know what, again, these things happen. Often it's a case of fat fingers on a mobile phone and when they have asked to unsubscribe the option to mark as SPAM has been so close as a "yes" and "no" option that they have accidentally done it.

If it's not accidental, then it's still ok!

Even if it's malicious it's ok.

As long as you aren't getting masses of people marking your emails as SPAM it's not going to cause you any difficulties and you know that you aren't spamming people or adding people to your list without their consent.

Make sure your emails are written directly for the people who you are best set to serve, fill them full of value and look after your subscriber list and you won't go far wrong.

Remember to respect the fact that people have given you permission to drop into their inbox, and as we are now much more protective of our email addresses then this is an honour indeed. Remember that!! Don't treat your fans like walking purses. Don't use your list to simply send sales emails.

How do you go about growing your email list? You need to concentrate on FANTASTIC free content that you can give away to your fans in exchange for their email address.

My biggest tips here are to know the problem which consumes your clients the most and they wake up seeking answers to AND get specific.

A woolly freebie that's very GENERAL won't attract masses of sign ups. SOLVE a specific problem that's bothering your fans.

How much should you include in there – enough to give your fans great value, a sample of how you work and your style BUT not so much that they will never come back for more from you.

Which format should you put your freebie in? An E-book? Audio? Video? Workbook? Checklist? Cheatsheet?

So many options!! I love a good checklist or cheat sheet as it always lets people see a fairly condensed version of what they need to, and who doesn't love ticking off a checklist? BUT the format isn't all that important, as lcng as it's a format that your crowd will consume, it's more about the title of that freebie and the content.

I have included the Freebies That Fly Ebook within the resources for this book which gives you ideas of the freebies you could include in yours, access it here >>> www.beabusinessrockstar.com

When you are putting together a freebie you MUST make sure that the delivery of that freebie is all automated and you don't need to get involved.

Make sure that you are happy that it's a good introduction to working with you and your business.

Remember – just because it's free to your audience you can't afford to just throw something together. The quality must be reflective of your business as a whole.

Your freebies are setting the expectation and standards of what people can expect when coming into contact with your business.

Growing your list needs to be something that is front of mind for you at all times. It needs to be something that you ask yourself daily. What can I do today in order to grow my list?

Content Marketing

She who shares the very best content wins (as long as she shares it with all her all)!

A Rockstar has a business which is content based. Your business is all about the content you create and therefore the marketing you are doing needs to showcase this content perfectly. Your content, whether that be free content or content that is in exchange for sign-ups or paid for content it doesn't really matter, it's all about the creation of great quality content.

I know that your business might not be based on marketing knowledge but you have to get good at marketing in order to be a Rockstar. It's a craft you'll need to hone. You'll do it your way but it will need an investment of time and (to a lesser extent) money in order to be a Grand Master Marketeer. Marketing isn't icky. It's not hard. It's about sharing your message.

Not only does your content allow you to continue to attract new people to your business and allow them to try you out for free and check that you are a good fit for them, it also enhances your credibility, reputation and all round awesomeness.

It's essential in the path of creating and nurturing relationships.

Your content runs through absolutely everything that you do. Your content can be your blogs, your webpages, your Facebook status updates, your tweets, your articles, your newsletter, your freebies – everything.

It's about you communicating with your audience. Your content allows you to have that consistency. It allows you to be popping up regularly for your fans and to ensure that they don't forget about you.

Content is the cornerstone of your business as it's everything that you produce.

When you are writing blogs you are creating a community, you are interacting with your fans, you are providing them with useful and relevant advice. You are also positioning yourself as an expert, strengthening the relationship that you are forming with your fans and providing value.

If you have written a list of topics which form part of your teachings or specialism within your Crowd Notebook then you can refer back to here in order to decide what you can blog about.

You can create this content in advance.

When I am in the mood for writing I can sit down and produce 10 blogs in one sitting. I don't just throw those blogs straight out there though.

They sit on my website, saved as drafts, so that I can use them as and when I need them. It means that if I have a week where I can't write for toffee then I have backups available that are ready to go.

Again, nothing needs to work in isolation. Your blogs can lead to one of your freebies and then can also be used to share on all of the different platforms you work on as well as be dissected to make other content.

Stay focused on what you can do in order to serve your crowd. I was talking to one lady at a networking event about writing for your fans and she said to me that she sits down at her table and she looks across the table and says to her fan (imaginary – I know, seems nuts but works) – what can I help you with today?

Some ideas to think about to take your content from good to awesome are:

Easy to share content – I have social sharing on all of my blogs (it's a simple Wordpress Plugin that allows my audience to share my blogs at the click of a button).

Ask people to do things. Create a call to action – if you want them to share your blog then ask them to share it, if you want them to comment and interact then ask them to, if you have a freebie that's relevant to the subject you are discussing then ask them to sign up for it. Keep your SEO in mind when you are creating web content. You want to drive traffic to your content but you would also like people to find you when they are searching internetty land for that particular subject.

Create something that people WANT to share.

When you are writing content PLEASE don't be all words. This week I clicked on someone's blog and I couldn't bear to read it, looking at the blog page made my head hurt. The font was small, the paragraphs were long and there were no breaks in the text for headings or pictures.

Make sure you:
- Go with a good title
- Break up your text with headings
- Use images to capture the eye
- Add a Social Sharing plugin
- Share your blog on your own Social Media Platforms.
- Optimise your blog for the search engines.
- Proofread it (or get someone else to – apparently the Grammar Police don't like mistakes!)
- Be Yourself

> "You can't edit a blank page."
>
> *Nora Roberts*

Marketing is about MUCH more than ramming sales messages down people's throats. When you ram sales messages down people throats all you will do is make them choke. You will make them disengage with you, you will make them feel like walking purses and you don't value them. I mean, you REALLY don't want that.

CHAPTER REMINDER CHECKLIST

Remember...

Marketing is about serving your fans and showing you at your shiniest

Avoid spewing out content for content's sake.

Focus your attention where your fans hang out.

Remember to get the best out of your content – not only looking at multiple platforms for sharing that content BUT also looking at the different ways you can use the content (e. video/audio/visual/written).

Video is King of Content – don't be afraid to try it.

8 ROCKSTAR PRODUCTS

I want you to know that your business can look and feel any way you want it to. That includes your product suite. I am going to let you into some of the ways that I have looked to help more people within my business and one of those ways that has been fundamental to setting me free to serve more people and make more money has been leverage.

Having a suite of products means that people can access your business at different price points, with differing levels of help and support from you.

Why Leverage Rocks

Let's talk about the why!

Why should you even begin to consider taking your ideas and turning them into an online business? Ok, so when you work one to one or face to face with clients one of two things happen – you eventually run out of time, you are so busy and your diary is so rammed full that you can't fit in another soul to see you this month. What this does it puts a MASSIVE ceiling on your earning potential. No more hours left to sell = no more money!

OR you struggle to find clients in your locality, you struggle to get people who want to pay for what you do or they want to pay a pittance, they don't respect you or your time and you feel like you are on a constant merry-go-round trying to find more and more clients, marketing your little heart out and only just managing to scrape by.

We don't want either of these situations.

I have worked with a lovely lady called Sarah. Sarah has a hypnotherapy business. She re-trained as a hypnotherapist after being made redundant. I am sure she won't mind me saying (and we do giggle about it now) SHE WAS CLUELESS as to what she needed to do to get her business going. She struggled through for over a year. She was forever fire-fighting, she was always broke and she was also doing 60 mile round trips to see one client, which took more than 3 hours out of her day and once she worked out her mileage costs those appointments were making her an absolute pittance.

She was REALLY stuck. She was REALLY broke.

Something had to change, and what changed was that she took her business online. She now has the makings of a SUPER successful business and is well on her way to being an absolute Rocksta. Just a couple of months into working together she launched her first programme and can now pay her rent with ease and buy her children treats – the pressure is off and it's now all about building that business to the SUPER SUCCESSFUL status.

concentrate on my one to one clients before I launch an online programme, I need to have a big list before I do anything online." That, my dear, is simply NOT true. You don't need to have a massive list in order to launch your online business. The trick is to grow your list whilst you launch. If you follow this advice then you fall into one of the two traps – you get too busy and your list building has to go on the back burner in any event OR you are too busy hustling for new one to one clients that your list building goes on the back burner. Either way you never grow that list. I know, it's pants! You are either the loser or you're the loser (no win/win in sight here!)

Time for money, that's what one to one work is – you give your time & people pay you money.

Time for money can also fall down for another couple of reasons, what happens if you can't work for any reason. What happens when your children or parents are poorly or you are ill. You then have to clear out your diary, you have to let lots of people down, you have to re-schedule everything, everything becomes a massive stress, you end up even busier than you were but you also have other demands on your energy, for example your caring duties for a poorly loved one, or you getting yourself better, and to top it all off you aren't making any money whilst you aren't working.

So let's talk about lovely leverage. I'm not a fan of the term "passive income" (to be totally honest the phrase pisses me off) because I think that for lots of people passive income conjures up images of you being able to do NOTHING at all and get paid MASSES for it. This isn't the case, you need to put the work in at the outset and then the income will be leveraged. Whether you sell that product once or a million times it won't need any extra work. You will have spent a set amount of time creating something and will be able to sell it over and over again.

Leveraged is exactly what a proportion of your products need to be. You will produce products and programmes with your knowledge and talent and you will be able to sell them to people all over the world, they will be able to buy and listen to your materials even when you are fast asleep in bed.

- It doesn't matter if you need a week off work.
- You can go on holiday and still make money
- There are no limits to the amount of money that you can make
- You don't need to juggle a diary rammed full of appointments with barely time to make a brew and have a wee between clients.
- You can work in the middle of the night unless that's your thing.
- You can work from home
- You can work from a café
- You can work anywhere in the world
- You can work around your children
- You can take time off without it having an impact on your income
- You can help more people
- You can help people all over the world
- The possibilities and earning potential are limitless

You might be striving for a global empire or you might want a business that provides you with flexibility, less stress and a good income. Your motives are personal. Your dreams and goals of what you want from your life and business are yours – think of them as the fuel for your business.   When you're having a bad day you can tap into your rocket fuel and propel off.

Fancy some of these benefits to fly into your world? A truly flexible business that can work to whatever schedule and rules that you decide? It's possible with an online leveraged business.

A special note to you if you're just starting your business journey...

If You're Starting From Scratch

Now is the time to start right! Firm foundations, structure and strategy will serve you well. Now is the time to make sure that you are starting to gather your fans around you – these fans are going to be people who bloomin' love what you do, the people you are best placed to help, the people who have problems that you can solve.

Start before you're ready. Spending time gathering your crowd before you have anything to sell to them is fine, in fact – it's perfect. That way you'll start from a place of value and giving.

Fancy business names? Do you need one, do you want one?

I have worked with people who have a name for their brand and people who work under their own name.

It doesn't really matter.

Your message and positioning are a zillion times more important than your business name. What is important is that if you are going to use a brand name that you most certainly and definitely DO NOT use it to hide behind that brand name. You MUST NOT use that brand name as protection and cover. That brand MUST resonate with your audience and MUST be connected to what it is that you do.

- Does it fit?
- Does it make sense?

One of my lovely clients had been working under a brand name for a little while. Her brand name did not reflect how her business had evolved and she was shyly hiding behind the brand. Lots of people who were in her network had no idea what she did. She was anonymous.

She came out! She came out, loud and proud and started to use her own name. She bought the website domain in her own name and built a brand around her.

This was her turning point for lots of success in her business. It had made her more visible.

She went on to achieve a 5 figure launch first time out.

At first it can be scary to be visible. It can cause endless worry about whether putting yourself out there is going to end up with negative feedback, and whether you are setting yourself up to be criticised and ridiculed. This is invariably a beast you have created in your head.

So it's time to look at your crowd of raving fans that you are going to be gathering around you and see how you can start to build products that they will love!!

You have forgotten how much you know!

The biggest reminder I have for you, when you are bringing together a leveraged product is that you have forgotten what it's like not to have the knowledge that you have. We take for granted that stuff we do without thinking about, the stuff that's kinda on auto pilot if you like.

You presume everyone has that knowledge and can do that thing. That presumption is wrong. It's only become second nature to you because you know how to do it and you've been through the tricky learning curve.

Chances are that a lot of the stuff you do without thinking is absolute GOLD!

ALWAYS remember – You've forgotten what you know. How much you know, the depth of your knowledge.

It comes to you with ease, you can do it on autopilot.

This is a reminder that everyone's specialist subject isn't the same AND the things that you find easy, others don't have a natural aptitude in.

I knock out Facebook Ads without any stress or physical/mental discomfort. I can do it without even thinking BUT I know that loads of people struggle with Facebook Ads. Because they come to me with ease I must continue to remind myself of how to take each step, what people need to think about and how to take them through it in a logical way.

I want you to go back to the basics, rewind right back to the beginning. It might be that you have had this special talent ever since you can remember or it might be that you can remember your own learning journey.

If your subject is one that you have been blessed with for as long as you can remember, then you need to put yourself in the shoes of someone who doesn't know anything about your subject.

Where do you even start with this one then? The starting point is a good, old fashioned BRAIN DUMP. It's time to get absolutely everything out of your head. Grab a brew (beverage of your choosing) and set to work. Give yourself an hour, with no filter whatsoever to get all of the information out of your head. You mustn't sensor yourself, don't think about whether it fits or not, whether it's appropriate or not. Just let it all flow out.

You might have reams and reams of paper with all of your ideas flooding through.

It might take you a couple of attempts at sitting down to do this.

If you are over-thinking it then it won't flow. You need to be completely open-minded and ready to let it all work through from your brain to your pen (or fingers if you are typing).

When I say that you need to get everything out I really do mean everything.

- Take a read through it.
- What's missing?
- Are there any gaps?
- Have you gone right back to basics?
- If your programme is crafted for a complete beginner – have you covered everything that you would need to tell a complete beginner?

Leave your notes, step away for a little while. Then, with fresh eyes you need to make some sense of your masses of notes that you prepared!

I bet when you look over it now some of it surprises you.

So you need to be looking for themes.

You need to be looking for things that will help people get unstuck.

If you already have a crowd or you have the beginnings of a crowd – perhaps you have a Facebook Page or Twitter followers then it might be worth your while asking them where they are stuck right now.

What is it that you could help them with?

You can either do this on social media or you can put together a little survey.

Top tip with surveys – make them super easy to complete & enter them into a prize draw (always nice to have the chance of winning a present in there for people to get actively completing them).

Try to have as many multiple choice questions as possible (you can put an "others – please state" box in there too in order to mop up more information). Multiple choice allows people to complete your survey quickly.

People are busy, make it easy for them to help you.

If you aren't in a position to ask the audience just yet then don't panic. Spend a little more time considering the subjects in question yourself.

Split your notes down into topics, the likelihood is that you will naturally see a number of topics jumping out of the paper at you, they may need breaking down again later but don't worry about that.

For the purposes of this book we are going to look at creating a class rather than a programme, so essentially you are only going to need to pick one topic and perhaps even just a subtopic.

What you need to start to think about here is – what will help them to move forward in their life/business.

You will NOT be able to solve all of their problems in a class BUT you will be able to help them to move forwards.

Once you work out what this is then you have your learning

objective – YAY!! You have the destination – their Town called Awesome.

What do you need to teach them in order to take them from the town called Stuck (where they are hanging out right now) through to the Town Called Awesome.

As I have explained before – I like to think of your classes and programmes as being a little bit like a Sally Sat Nav (don't judge me for my Sat Nav having a name – Sally Sat Nav lives in Betty Blue Our Beautiful Fiat 500 for our Awesome Adventures). Anyway, I digress.

Ok, so people could go on this journey on their own but the likelihood is that without the directions they are going to get lost, they may well meander off onto the side roads, get stuck behind a tractor and go off in a big route and loop back to the start (or the scenic route as my dad used to call the weird direction routes << read getting lost >> in my childhood).

Your programme will take them directly on the motorway.

Your learning points might be little service stations on that motorway breaking up the journey.

Here's a little Rockstar Route that might help you plot that journey from Stuck to Awesome and will start to get you thinking about the points along the way, the stuff your crowd will need to learn in order to pass through without getting stuck or overwhelmed.

>>>>>>>>>>>>>>>>>>>>>>

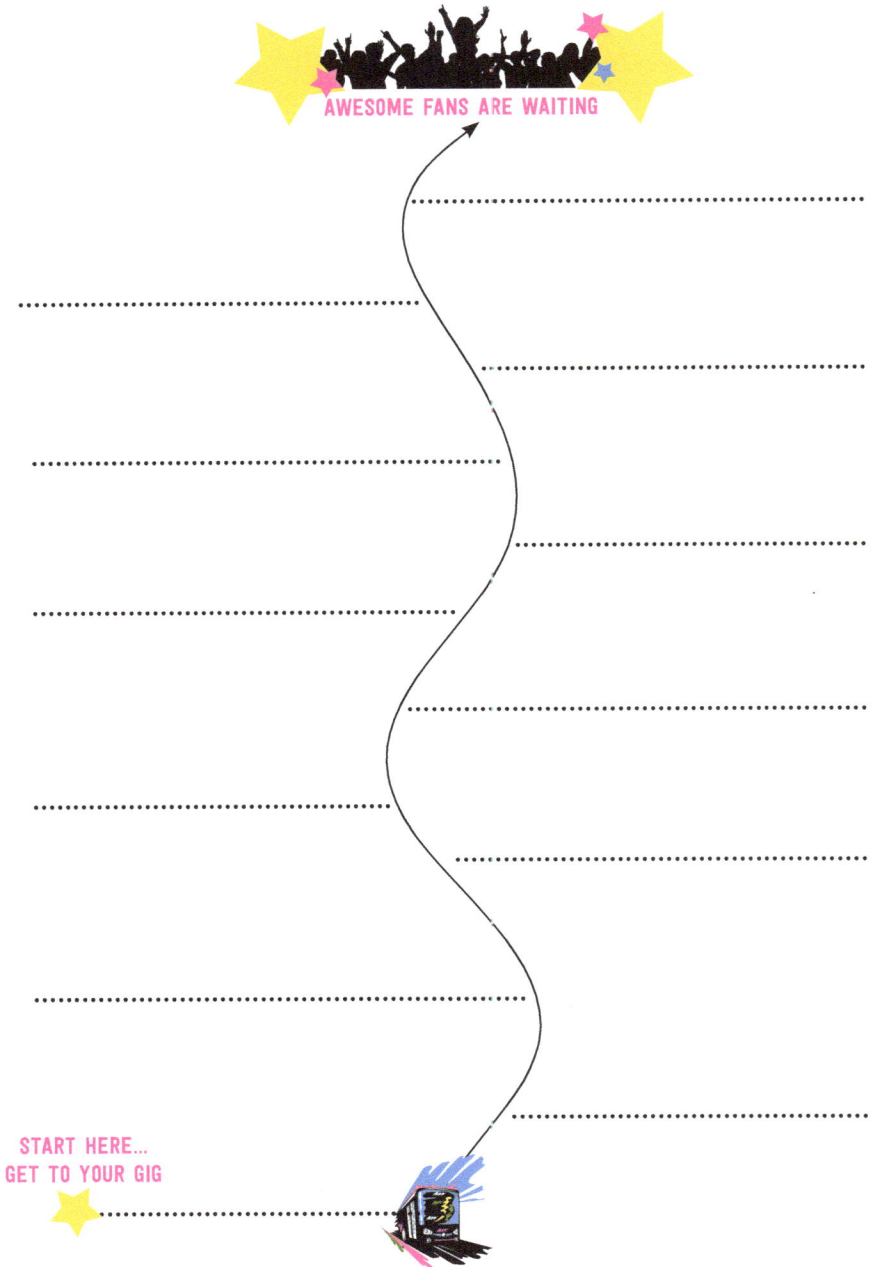

AWESOME FANS ARE WAITING

START HERE...
GET TO YOUR GIG

The next stage is to flesh it out – I want you to write down the topic you have chosen and then make a list of all the things that you could talk about that fall within that topic (AND I MEAN EVERYTHING – no censoring here again).

Now it's time to run one of my VERY favourite mantras – JUST BECAUSE I COULD DOESN'T MEAN I SHOULD.

The BIGGEST mistake I see playing out over and over again when people are bringing together a leveraged product is the need to get all the information that they know in there. It's a quest to prove you know your stuff. It's a quest to add stacks of value BUT be careful as it might just throw you off course.

You don't want to overwhelm people with information. When you are bringing together a class you can't load it full of masses and masses of information, 1001 learning points and a gazillion tasks for them to carry out – that would be madness. It would leave your crowd overwhelmed. You will paralyse them into inaction. If they can't process and implement then they can't progress.

You need to think about the level that your product will be aimed at. Is it a beginner level and they know nothing about the subject whatsoever? << Here you need to think about the foundations. If you are expecting them to already have a foundation knowledge then they may well be the intermediates and you need to work out what they need from you in order to make progress, OR you might want to help people to really SUPERCHARGE their life/biz, again – what would they need to make that happen?

I think that a class is best broken down to about 3-5 learning points.

Take the information that you want to include and write it down on post- it notes (this works really well for both classes and programmes). Once you have the topics to cover down on post it notes then add an intro and a conclusion to your post it note pile. Obviously, the intro is going to go at the beginning. This is where you are going to talk about who this product is for and what it's all about. The conclusion will take up the tail and this will be where you round up your learning points and any action steps that people need to take after finishing the class.

The remaining post it notes need to be brought together into an order which makes sense. Sometimes this is very natural and organic and other times it takes some thinking about.

The great thing with the post it notes is that you can keep moving them about until it sits right.

I always suggest that once you feel like you've cracked it then you leave it for a few hours before coming back to them with a clear mind and double check the running order.

Products come in all sorts of shapes and sizes, programmes come in all shapes and sizes.

Products can be:
- A quick video
- A big, looooong class that you just pop out there for all to view
- A live call

- A pre-recorded class
- A series of recorded classes
- A series of live classes

Gosh, the choices are endless – no wonder it becomes a source of procrastination.

OK, time to go through it and make some decisions.

Who Is The Product Aimed At?

Remember to check back to your who!

Now it's time to work out EXACTLY who your product is directed towards. It's no good at all deciding to do a live class at 10am in the morning if your crowd are likely to be at work at that time. It's not a great decision to put together a SUPER LONG call if your crowd are busy – they won't have time to consume it.

Not only will it help you judge how you should deliver your call and the length of your product, BUT it'll also help you to write the call and bring together copy for the sales page if your intention is to get people to sign up for the product.

I have found that my lovely crowd prefer me to break down my products. Once upon a time I would have knocked out 1 hour long classes without much thought (some even getting up to the 90 min mark) BUT then I realised that that required my lovely clients having to carve out huge periods of time within their day.

The solutions – bite-sized chunks. Each post it note would become a short video.

What Do You Want To Cover?

Getting clear on your message and exactly what you want to share with your crowd. Remember, you have the old curse of knowledge/you have forgotten how much you know and it might be that you jump straight in at a higher level than your crowd are able to digest. It's important that you take your topic back to basics. If you wade in at a very high level (unless it's clear that your product is put together for people with a foundation knowledge already) you will end up scaring your audience witless!

It's tempting when you start out to add every single piece of information that you know about every single subject into your programme content.

It might be that deep down you feel you need to prove your knowledge.

It might be that you want to make your programme incredible value (you can do this without overstuffing it)

It might be that you just don't know what to cut out.

The result?

THE ONE thing we need to avoid at all costs - overwhelm for your crowd and a product which they just can't use because there's too much there, they have no idea what to do or where to start.

An inability for you to sell anything else to your audience.

My recommendation, for the very first product that you bring together is that you record your class with the use of a slide presentation. It's means that you don't have to spend time worrying about the whole face to camera thing. It means that there is less chance of you procrastinating and worrying about how you look, how much you gesticulate and whether you are prone to pulling funny faces. Slides also make sure that you stay on topic, that you don't get distracted and that you don't lose your train of thought.

All in all slides will keep you on the right path and make sure that you have less to worry about – which is perfect for your first time out.

Live Classes

Note – they can go wrong – but it can happen to anyone.

I've had a few corkers!!

I had scheduled a live class. It was quite an intensive class and I had prepared slides to walk people through exactly what it was that I was teaching. I had a tech fail as we went live and the presentation wouldn't share with the audience and I had to teach the whole class, without knowing in advance as a face to camera class. I was grateful that even though they couldn't see my slides I was still able to see that at this end but it did make me much more mindful throughout the presentation of how I was presenting myself as well as presenting the class.

I'm totally used to presenting live and the whole introduction of live streaming has seen to the fact that being live is super comfortable (once you get the hang of it).

I think that what is important when you are looking at presenting anything live is to unclench a little. Anything could happen. That's not permission to sit and worry about every possible outcome and what may or may not happen – it's not about expecting curve balls, it's just about knowing that they are possible and not getting too hung up and what happens along the way.

How do you get your offering right?

You need to get really clear about who your product is for. You may well have defined who your crowd is, what they are struggling with and how it is that you help them BUT you need to take it one step further when you are putting together programme content.

You will have a sub niche of your crowd who would be interested in this programme.

- Is it a beginner, intermediate or advanced programme?
- Are you expecting them to have any foundation knowledge before taking this programme?
- What outcomes are you leading your crowd towards if they take this programme?
- Will it deal with a specific issue that your crowd struggle with?

Think about the journey that your crowd are going to be taken on by your product, think about how you will take them from their stuck place and what they will have achieved/be able to do/been able to implement by the end of your programme. You need to think about your programme as a journey and what steps they will need in order to complete that journey with ease.

Look at breaking down your content so that you are providing 3-5 learning points per piece of programme content (max).   If you are bombarding your crowd with lots of different ideas, strategy and learning points in one go then the likelihood is that they won't be able to implement any of it.

You want your content to be SUPER useful to your crowd and to allow them to make the biggest difference possible.

Write down what you are going to teach them within your programme or class and write down where your crowd are stuck right now. Work backwards from there in order to see that you are providing them with the steps that they need to move forwards, and to get to that end outcome that you envisage. This will give you a good idea as to the content which needs to be included in your programme.

Make sure that you are covering each of the steps that they will need to take logically.   Can you provide checklists to help them work through the content logically?

Mindmap the subjects that you will include in your programme to get your crowd the outcomes that you envisage from your programme, and that will be the start of you bringing together your programme structure.

Remember the post it note exercise – that one's priceless and will REALLY help you to get that order right.

Be mindful that you need enough programme content to allow your crowd to achieve the desired outcomes and move forwards with their life or business BUT not too much that it stops you putting together a more advanced programme, or that your programme content is too much and it overwhelms your crowd.

Make sure your slides are great prompts to help you to work through that content and that they allow you to flow.

There is nothing worse than listening to someone read word for word from a slide presentation. People don't need that.

Remember to have room for examples – people learn much more when they are shown about the practical application of the theory in the real world.

Break the presentation up with images.

Make sure you spend some time checking that you are happy with your presentation because you are going to record this!!

Do you need to rehearse it? I don't rehearse my presentations but I have some clients who do a couple of run-throughs before they go live. It all depends on what feels most comfortable for you. As I take my time preparing my presentations I am confident that I have already captured the flow of what I'm going to say.

On your first time out you might want to have a couple of run-throughs so you know that, as soon as you press that big red record button, know exactly what you are going to say.

Do you need to script your class? Again, that depends, I often find it difficult to listen to scripted classes that are presented badly. Some people can read from a script and pull it off. Others, not so much so, you can tell it's scripted.

I find that the prompts and cues on my slides are enough to take me through what I need to include. I also print off my slides and have little notes on them in case there is anything additionally I need to make sure I include at certain points, and little notes about the stories and anecdotes I intend to tell.

The above gives you an outline of how you can start to bring together products within your business BUT let me give you some pointers I have learned along the way:

- It's important that you don't blow all of your knowledge in 1 product. It's bloomin' overwhelming for you AND your fans.
- Don't continually create MORE and MORE products. It's important that you don't have TOO MANY choices for people as what will end up happening is that they will have no idea as to which is the best product for them and then they'll end up buying nothing. You won't have the marketing bandwidth to do a plethora of products justice either. Products will end up being neglected within your marketing plans and you won't be giving them the best opportunity to help the people they are here to help.
- Think about which product you want to be famous for? Which one is your signature product?

- Think about your products as part of your suite of services. During My Project 100k I had the following services:
    - Business Consultancy and Management
    - VIP Clients
    - Programmes (higher and lower level)
    - Classes

That suite of products allowed people to work with me at different levels for different levels of investment.

A word on subscription products – monthly membership clubs and the likes. I know that lots of people look on at people building membership clubs in awe. They are the product which keeps paying. They are fabulous for securing your income over the longer term BUT they aren't a super easy option. I know that I never included a membership product into my product suite for a couple of years because I wanted to make sure that the subscription product would be worth my time and effort and that I was in the best place to serve my crowd. People are naturally suspicious of subscriptions. Most of us have taken out memberships that we have never used and are much more cautious about signing up for things on a subscription basis – even if we are able to cancel them immediately.

So, whilst they are AMAZING to include in your product suite my advice is usually that you need to make sure you have built your crowd and following sufficiently before embarking on this product type.

CHAPTER REMINDER CHECKLIST

Remember...

Leveraging your time is crucial if
you want to grow your business.

Think about the kind of leveraged
income you could generate.

Don't underestimate the depth of your knowledge

Overstuffing your products (albeit with great value)
will scare your audience.

Get clear on who your product is
for before you start writing.

Always, always, always have plenty of post it notes.

9 LAUNCH
LIKE A ROCKSTAR

Let's talk LAUNCH!

Let's talk about what it's like in real life to launch!

Ok, so launching ain't for the fainted hearted BUT the results you will get are massively worth all the time, effort, sweat, wobbles and tears that will go into a launch.

If you don't launch your products and programmes then you aren't giving yourself the best chance of success. If you don't launch you leave money on the table. If you don't launch then you aren't helping as many people with your zone of genius as you should be.

Launch = helping more people + making more money.

No brainer then really isn't it?

So let's take a look at some of the (very funny) launch stories of some of my wonderful clients...

Once you have done your first one and seen the results you will be dying to do it again, I promise!

Kate's story... **Once you have done your first one and seen the results you will be dying to do it again, I promise!**

> 66

"Launching is scary and it takes a lot of determination and energy BUT the rewards are like nothing else... if you do it right. There's no way of dressing it up, you'll worry about the doorbell ringing and you will feel like you are desperate for the toilet the second you go live – no matter how many times you have been! You'll doubt yourself and you will fluff your lines, and you'll get all flustered BUT you will be getting your message out to people who need it, and building your list and making money. There is no other way to make this kind of money and create this kind of awesome in your business in my opinion! You so need to swallow your fear and get out of your own way, have another wee then LAUNCH!!!

And once you have done your first one and seen the results you will be dying to do it again, I promise!

Even if you need to do it with Diocalm / Prozac – it's bloody worth it! That bit's a joke by the way!"

Kate Spencer. Practical Spirituality Coach
www.kate-spencer.com

Gilly's story... **Why On Earth Didn't I Believe In Myself?**

> 66
>
> "Launching is like vomiting! Just before you do it you really don't want to do it!! You get a bit freaked out. You feel icky in your stomach. You think you might even die. Your mouth is dry and your brain is fried. You suddenly realise that your product is rubbish. The vomit rises. Something in your soul urges you to breathe and in a moment of madness you hit SEND. The bile rises horribly and you try to distract yourself. Then... you hear the ping, ping, ping of emails from PayPal advising you of people rushing to grab your early bird offer and you punch the air! Why on earth didn't I believe in myself?"
>
> *Gilly Woodhouse*
> **Business Coaching for Osteopaths**

Emma's story... **I would describe the whole process as scary, exhilarating and nerve wracking, a mixture of emotions, but, at the end of it all, it is so worth it.**

66

"My launch story! When I think of launching I think of a rocket – and that is exactly what it is like... There is lots of prep to get it ready, lots of behind the scenes activity which no one sees, then, you "initiate launch sequence" and your butt is on fire and you are flying up, up and up and you daren't look down – you just have to keep looking at where you want to get to!! I am a newbie to launching, I have launched twice. Both with the awesome help of Emma.

My launches have been successful but, each and every time I have felt a bit (actually a lot!) like I am winging it. I kind of have a plan, but I also kind of just jump in with two feet and get on with it. Because if I didn't do that, I would probably still be planning out my programme!!

Launching is scary. I have had the wobbles, I get to the point where I feel like I can't promote it anymore, I get the overwhelm feeling. BUT, each time I have just kept going and it always comes good.

I would describe the whole process as scary, exhilarating and nerve wracking, a mixture of emotions, but, at the end of it all, it is so worth it.

I would describe the whole process as scary, exhilarating and nerve wracking, a mixture of emotions, but, at the end of it all, it is so worth it. I am loving what I am doing, the people I am helping with my programmes. Launching an online biz is so worth it, but in order to succeed you have to have the right support. Emma has genuinely been a critical element to the success of my launches. I am learning new things every day and I know my next launch will be even better because of the support and encouragement that I get from Emma and the other wonderful ladies in Emma's programme. If you are considering launching, my advice? Publicly announce a launch date and get on with it...
you'll never look back."

Emma Etheridge
Wedding Biz Bootcamp

Before we dive any further into launching here is a great quote from the wonderful Marie Forleo...

> **"**
>
> "If you have a product or service that you believe in and you don't do everything to market the heck out of it, you are stealing from those who need it the most."
>
> *Marie Forleo*

Launching online can be a daunting task. It can feel initially like you are going to go off and shout into a deep, dark hole and doubt starts to creep in about whether you will ever be in a positon to pull off big launches and make money from your online products. Add to that the worry about whether anyone will buy from you or not, and add a sprinkling of whether or not your product is good enough, you can see yourself in a massive sea of doubt, procrastination and fear!

So, what are you to do? Give up?

Certainly not! What you are to do is to bring together a launch plan and strategy that will work for both you and your business. It will be bespoke! It's no good working super hard on a launch and it not sitting right with you and your business because this will not attract flocks of customers.

On a little side note, this certainly doesn't mean that a launch will be inside your comfort zone because, sorry (not sorry), it won't. A launch will always stretch you and when you are stretching outside of your comfort zone that's when the magic is happening and your business is growing.

So, what's it take to pull off an awesome launch?

Let's go over the steps!

Re-cap Steps

Work Out Your Zone of Genius

This is where you need to start! Right at the beginning. You might say "oh but I know what my niche is" and then proceed to give me a sketchy outline of the most massive sector imaginable. Your Zone of Genius is a little different, think about it as your Mastermind Specialist Subject. It is something that comes to you naturally, you can teach people about it with ease and you would be more than happy to talk about it all day long. There is a change in your voice when someone asks you about it, a fire lights in your belly. You want to share that knowledge and help people to conquer the skill.

Work Out Who You Serve & What Journey You Take Them On

This is all about who can benefit most from your Zone of Genius.

Who is it that would get the greatest benefit from whatever it is that you teach?

Think about where you would be if you didn't have that Zone of Genius, where would you be stuck, where could you not make any progress?

Would you be missing out on opportunities? Losing money?

Miserable? Would you feel stuck and frustrated?

I like to think of it as you need to be taking your audience on a journey, you need to be taking them from their Stuck Place to their Awesome Place and when you come around to productising your Zone of Genius then that product will essentially be their Sally Sat Nav. It will be the quickest possible route for them from stuck to awesome. You will create their motorway. Yes, these are things that they could probably achieve themselves, eventually. They could go out and do lots of work and wade through zillions of free resources available online, they would probably wander off onto the B-Roads, they would detour and might even end up back where they started.

BUT you can show them the easy way!

Build a Crowd of Raving Fans

You need to start to gather an audience around you of the people that would benefit most from your Zone of Genius. The first step is to pick a platform in order to gather that crowd. It might be that it's a Facebook Page or your Twitter feed or a networking group. It should be a place where your crowd are most likely to hangout and a place where you are comfortable in hanging out too.

Nurture That Crowd of Raving Fans

Once you start to build that crowd that it's your job to make sure that you look after them well. You need to be sharing really great, valuable content with them on a regular basis. You need to be offering them free resources and showing them the ways you can help them.

Get Them on Your List

Your list is one of the most valuable assets in your business. If you don't translate your crowd from observers into subscribers then you will be missing out on helping people and building your business. Your list is important because it allows you to drop into people's inboxes on your terms, when you have something to tell them. If you don't have a list then you also miss the opportunity of getting in touch with your crowd should anything (touching wood, touching wood) ever happen to your social media platforms.

Design a Product They Will Fall Over Themselves For

This is all about taking your Zone of Genius, adding your fans' majoring sticking points and creating a product that takes them to awesome.

Setting Out On The Launch Path

Plant the seeds - before you set off into Launch Mode you need to make sure that you have started to plant the seeds with your crowd about what you have got coming and how it may well just change their world. Tell them about the product you are working on and whether it's something that will be of interest to them. Think about when Apple release information about a new device, they do this months before it's ready for market and people start to get hyped about it. Another industry that does this really well is the movie industry. They tell you about their new movie months/years in advance and start to plant the seeds with trailers and clips, they start to hook you in and start to make you feel like their movie is already familiar and therefore you will want to see it.

Decide On a Launch Strategy

You need to pick a launch strategy that works for you but also for your audience. There is no point in you deciding that you will purely market your product to your list when in fact your list is tiny, and even if they all bought it will never bring you the returns that you would want from your offering.

Nail an Early Bird

Eeeekkk – that sounds cruel doesn'- it! This is you offering your crowd a discounted price for getting involved in your product early. It allows you to start to make money from your product whilst marketing it and lets you br'ng urgency and scarcity to your launch on more than one occasion – quick, quick or you'll miss this offer. When you are first starting out in developing online products or programmes it's a great addition to a launch strategy. It might be an early bird or it might be an introductory offer. It's something I advocate as you start out so that you can have an injection of confidence as buyers are more likely to pay attention.

I still use introductory offers for new products or programmes but I don't change the prices on my other offerings throughout the launch process anymore. I have made a strategic decision that right now that's not working for me! I've decided to keep my knickers up when it comes to pricing. I don't want people having paid different prices for the same thing.

Market Like You Mean It

Whispering about your launch just won't cut it – you have to market like you mean it!

Perfect Your Pitch and Shift Your Selling Mindset

Selling is not icky! Selling is you offering people an opportunity to work with you further. Shift that mindset right away!

Get Over the Wobbles

Everyone experiences the launch wobbles at some point during their launch. You need to accept them for what they are – just a wobble and be safe in the knowledge that the wobble will pass!

Don't Give Up

Launch fatigue will hit, when you are launching it's a really intense period of marketing, promotion and generally a really busy period in your business. Make sure you keep going until the end and at the end, give yourself a lovely rest and BIG treat!

The first launch can be SUPER DUPER exciting and you can get caught up on the crest of the wave.

BUT... **RELAUNCH**

It should be really easy... shouldn't it? Relaunching a programme should be an absolute no brainer and it should be super easy to do. For heaven's sake, you've done it all before, the hard bit is done, you have created the programme and ran it once so it should be super easy to do again.

The problem is that it's not always as easy to relaunch a programme as you think. What often ends up happening is that you unintentionally cut corners and become complacent. You are not in the same zone with the programme as you were the first time round.

It doesn't have to be this way (pinky promise). Here is my relaunch formula, a guide on how to relaunch (that I use with my VIP clients) to nail a Rockstar Launch on a programme you have already had out there.

The key is in the preparation.

Start at the beginning. Start talking about the programme on your social media, start to raise people's curiosity about what's to come. Make it exciting and something that they truly don't want to miss out on.

If you didn't do this during/at the end of the last launch then collate all of the marketing materials that you used last time. Take a little bit of time to think about (but don't dwell on) what worked and what didn't work last time.

Re-Visit the Programme

Take some time to re-familiarise yourself with the programme. I know lots of people question whether their programmes are good enough/whether they need anything adding or whether they need to do things different UNTIL they look at it with fresh eyes and go - "do you know what, that programme is pretty awesome".

Reacquainting yourself with the programme will get your creative juices flowing again and reignite your passion for the content.

You can also update or make any revisions necessary at this stage.

Ask For Testimonials

You have run this programme before so if you haven't already done so then now is the time to get feedback from those who have taken part.

Update the Sales Page

You need to make some tweaks and amendments to the sales page, look at adding those testimonials/the social proof that it worked.

Update the Pricing

Make any tweaks to the wording that you need. The chances are that you know your crowd a little better since the last launch of the programme, you have seen first-hand the things that your current customers where struggling with. You can make this copy MUCH more compelling this time around.

- Check Everything Is Still Set Up (all systems are in place and still working).

- Are your payment portals still in place?
- Do you have your purchases linked to any automation that you might need?
- Think About The Live Call (if you intend to do them as part of your launch process)
- Are you going to run a live call (or a few calls) as part of your launch process?

Live calls are a great way of connecting further with your audience and crowd.   If you are going to do a live call then think about your subject. It needs to be compelling. It needs to be a subject that your audience want to know more about but also that will be a perfect lead in to your programme. You can add a short pitch in your live call and encourage sign ups with "action taker" offers.

So if you are going to do the free call then now's the time to:
- schedule in the dates
- set up the lists in your email system
- set up the auto responders
- set up the web page to host the live call
- set up the sign up page for the live call and link it to the list
- schedule emails to your list promoting the live calls
- schedule your promotions on Social Media to fill the seats on the live call.
- prepare your Early Bird

If you want to start your launch with a bang then it's time to set out with an Early Bird offer.   This is the perfect way to get an influx of sales right at the beginning of your launch process, it starts the cash flowing, it's the perfect way to get your crowd's interest sparked at the outset.

When it comes to launching it's important to think of quality not quantity. Zooming through a launch can mean that you don't engage as many people as you'd like as they haven't seen your marketing messages or you haven't had an opportunity to build or nurture a relationship with them.

Equally, a launch without urgency and scarcity will leave the door open for people to make purchases on their terms and won't compel them to press that buy button.

The urgency and scarcity needs to be genuine and authentic. People will be compelled to buy if they fear missing out, if they are going to be in the same position and not have the benefit of what you're offering. It may be that you have limited numbers that you are going to sell or a limited time deal. Whatever you use in order to encourage people to make decisive action, make sure that it's honest and that you aren't being disingenuous in the urgency and scarcity stakes.

CHAPTER REMINDER CHECKLIST

Remember...

Launching like a Rockstar is the only way to launch.

Leave that comfort zone behind and get ready to showcase your talent to the world.

DO NOT GIVE UP!

Get set for the Relaunch.

Quality launches are much more successful than Rushed ones.

10 MAKE MONEY LIKE A ROCKSTAR

I know most people would say that they do not run their business purely for the money & that is good. Money as a motivator can be quite fickle.

I went to a ladies' networking meeting a while back and the guest speaker was talking all about stress. Her promises were not to take our stress away or make us better but to empower us to recognise and deal with stress.

The first task was to dart around the room and brainstorm what causes us stress. The main protagonists were husbands, children, lack of time, too much to do, overwhelm & having high standards which only perfection would help to achieve. Out of over a dozen women not one person mentioned the word MONEY. Is that because everyone in that room was rolling in money [I don't think that is the answer]? Or because they were all being terribly British and not mentioning the M word? Or do we all genuinely not feel that money is a stress when placed directly against other things in our life.

I am not being flippant about money here because I know that lots of people have money worries and that worry can eat away at you. I get that, I've been there BUT the ladies in this group weren't putting it as a top stress factor in their world.

There were very personal stress triggers for some ladies, stress triggers that a lot of the other members of the audience could not relate to, stress about cutlery not being in its correct place in a kitchen drawer, stress that towels are not stacked correctly or tins are not standing to attention with their labels facing forwards in the cupboard. Even if you cannot resonate with these things, they can cause people masses of stress. You could see one lady's anxiety in her face as she discussed the feelings she got when things weren't "just so".

Now don't get me wrong, money (or lack of money) can cause massive stress in people's worlds. Financial hardship can be soul destroying, guilt inducing and lead to a mass of really difficult situations to deal with.

We all want/need to be financially abundant, money allows us choice, it allows us to be able to do things that we want to do, it allows us freedom and can help us to achieve ultimate wellbeing.

But, it seems from these ladies it is not something (unless your lack is so great) that we deem as one of our major stress factors in life.

This is not permission for you not to think of the money. The money is VITAL. Business is about making money.

You MUST think and talk about money. Money is not icky and evil. Money is fantastic.

A business that doesn't think about money is merely a hobby.

You HAVE TO get comfortable with managing your money. It will allow you to see what's working and make adjustments before there are any issues. I know when you first start out that you are prepared to just do a happy dance every time you receive a payment. You daren't even consider planning financially for the long term. You are reactive and this means that you end up falling into hustling patterns. You are chasing the next penny. There is no thought going into your long term income plans.

You might be tempted to cut corners and look for the quick buck. If you are doing this you will end up undervaluing yourself, your business and your fans.

A lot of the money-making activity in your business revolves around Sales Pages. You will drive your fans over to your sales pages and offer them an opportunity (note what I said there – offer & opportunity – big words to remember when it comes to selling and why it's not in the least bit icky).

Let me tell you a little bit about the biggest factors that I see missing from sales pages;

Why should I care?

What are you going to do for me?

Why should I work with you?

Three simple enough questions. Three questions that might pop you immediately on the back-foot BUT I certainly don't mean it that way. These questions are a little test that you should run on all of your sales copy.

Lots of people get caught up in the cuff and fluff, they get caught up in the what you'll get and how it's delivered, they get caught up in the stuff that doesn't really matter.

What people want to know is RESULTS!

What results will I get? What will I be able to do after taking your course or watching your video or signing up for your freebie? How are you going to change my world?

WORD OF CAUTION – don't make it up, don't make it pie in the sky, don't overpromise & under deliver.

My philosophy in all that I do is to be 100% transparent and make sure that what I promise is realistically achievable – yes, you won't get any of the results if you don't put any of the work in but it's certainly attainable.

How can you show results with the highest of integrity? Don't get caught in the whole – in 2 hours fortnightly you can be a millionaire kinda approach.

Yes, unfortunately, it catches attention and people are running after the next promise and the person who has the #1 secret (sssshhh <<< remember, there isn't one!!) AND for my fans they see lots of people telling them that they can make massive shifts in their business without doing any work. What is the "usual" approach in your niche? What's the overinflated, egotistical promise?

Be realistic with what you are promising, be transparent and clear BUT whatever you do keep your eyes on RESULTS when you are writing your sales copy.

A really good way to show changes to people's worlds is the use of testimonials and case studies – people are much more likely to believe someone else telling them that you are awesome rather than you telling them (they know you are going to say that anyway!)

Another good philosophy to employ is less I and Me – more You & We!

⭐ My Rockstar challenge to you is...

To take a look at your copy this week and check whether or not you are actually focusing on any results in what you are telling people?

Remember – sales pages are the window display of your business, they are the attraction point to draw people in. Your sales page should surprise and delight, ignite curiosity and make people self-select.

- A good shop window catches your eye.
- A good shop window allows you to identify whether there is stuff inside that shop that you would be interested in (or not).
- A good shop window is intriguing and makes you want to find out more, much much more.
- A window dresser does not just ram everything possible into the shop window, they do not overload the space

and bombard the customer. They are selective. They make it look nice.

- Time, energy and money is put into shop windows by major retailers, they hire window dressers to produce beautiful displays because they know that it will make them more money.
- How is your shop window for your products looking?

Obviously a new product needs a new sales page but it is also important that you periodically pop in there and check, update, tweak and amend the sales pages which you have done in the past.

If you have your sales pages sat on your website then a great tool in order to track whether or not those pages are working is to track your visitors to that page. You can do this via Google Analytics or a plugin on your website. It will let you know then if stacks of people are visiting the page. If you are achieving traffic to the page but you're not getting any purchases then there is something not working on your page, there is a mismatch.

I work through 13 magic ingredients below but the first, broad-brush, look at a sales page needs to be;

Recognition – allow them to recognise themselves early within the text of the page, is this for them? Should they invest the time to keep reading?

Empathy – show them that you understand where they are right now. Remember that town called Stuck? Show them that you get what it's like to be there.

What's it all about – give some details about what you are offering for sale.

Price – I'm an advocate of including the price.

What will it allow them to BE, DO, HAVE or ACHIEVE? Set out the promise – if they take the information you give them and they implement it all what's the end results?

Call to Action – what do you want them to do?

Why you – who are you and why should they choose to spend their money with you? You might also include your social proof in here.

So let's now look at the ingredients to add onto this framework..

13 Magic Ingredients to Sales Pages That Sell

- Your sales page needs to be written for your ideal client (really get under their skin and empathise with them here).
- Your sales page must be written from the heart – start with a super passionate piece of writing about why your programme is amazing and you can use that as the basis of the page as you go through the other elements.
- Your sales page needs to resonate with your ideal client.
- Your sales page needs to highlight your ideal client's problems, anxieties and fears.
- Your sales page needs to show people how to solve those problems.
- Your sales page needs to let people know what your

clients will get for their money and what the outcomes will be (how will it change their life or their business?).

- Your sales page needs a price.
- Your sales page needs a rousing call to action.
- Your sale page needs to be broken down so that it's not all words. Lots and lots of text is very difficult on the eye – use headings and images to break it up.
- Your sales page needs good images/visuals.
- Your sales page needs to reflect you and your personality.
- Your sales page needs social proof (great, awe-inspiring testimonials, results that people want to emulate).
- Make sure that you have answered the most popular questions you think your ideal client may have about this product. Address their objections. Bold – yes! But it's important that you get inside their head and know what might be holding them back from making the purchase. If you address this stuff straight away then that fleeting objection doesn't become a massive big sticking point for them.

There is no magic recipe to a sales page but a list of essential ingredients, a framework if you like, which you need to use to write your sales pages with.

The MOST essential element is to keep your ideal client in mind. If your client is ridiculously time poor then a massive long sales page is a waste of time, they won't have time to read it, they will either click away or scroll through just reading the headings and searching out the price (now that is a big bad waste of your efforts). If your ideal client is anxious about investing money then a short snappy sales page will just not cut the mustard.

You will find some fab resources to help you to craft your sales pages in the bonuses accompanying this book - www.beabusinessrockstar.com

Don't be afraid to tweak your sales page either. Once it is done it is not done forever, it needs a little bit of attention every now and then.

If you are really, really stuck in writing your sales pages you have three options:-

1. You are either just standing in your own way and you just need to get on and get it done – stop procrastinating.
2. You can take a look around internetty world and seek inspiration from other people's sales pages (don't copy – that's not cool – merely use it as inspiration!).
3. You can outsource them to a copy writer (but make sure that the essence of you and your personality is not lost).

Remember – putting maximum effort into your sales page will mean you can reap the results in sign-ups!

A final top tip for writing a sales page is, if the words just aren't coming for you then dictate your sales page. Record yourself talking about your programme. You're much more likely to capture the passion that way.

People are buying into more than the product. They are buying into the desired outcome and how your product can help to change their world. Make sure you are getting this across in your sales messages.

Be super clear on who your products are for (and who they are not for).

Tackle objections head on too – what might it be that's stopping your fans from buying? Address these issues and not only will it show your audience that you get them and the position that they are in but you can also be dealing with those objections at source.

ALWAYS REMEMBER

Make the process of buying from you easy for your fans. Make sure that they can find what they need and the process is super simple.

Pricing

Eeeeekkkkk, this one might bring you out in a cold sweat – pricing is just a difficult one because it brings up stacks of stuff around self-worth. It makes you put a price tag on your expertise.

Let's just get some stuff straight here – it's often the case that the more you charge, the more people value you. Now, I'm not talking about poking people's eyes out (overpricing and sat laughing at the naivety of your crowd – that's bad and that's wrong) here but I just want you to put this into perspective – often when things are cheap we start to think that there must be a catch, that's it's too good to be true, that it's rubbish quality. You don't want people thinking that about working with you now do you?

You also don't want to attract people who make decisions based on price alone. There is no loyalty with purse/price shoppers and more often than not they become the most difficult clients to deal with.

If all the doors are exactly the same and only the prices are different then you are going to head to the cheapest door. You don't want to get caught up in that kinda guy. Make your door different and the pricing isn't then comparative to other doors.

Your fans will value you and your time and will pay for that value accordingly. They WANT to be part of your stuff and as long as they can afford it they will jump in; their first consideration is NOT the price.

Pricing is predominantly about confidence.

Most people are undercharging! – FACT

Don't be afraid to be premium. Don't be afraid to stake your claim. Make sure that the quality of your stuff is epic and that you are over delivering and you won't go far wrong, even with premium prices.

> "
> "There is a simple but powerful rule: always give people more than they expect to get."
> *Nelson Baswell*

Make sure you are positioning yourself and your products correctly.

Think about how your fans can save time, save money, make more money, eliminate stress and have a happier time just for the price of your course – what is that worth to them? You are their shortcut, their supercharge, their chance at BIG results.

Think these through:

- Get out of your comfort zone with your pricing
- Remember that you are an expert
- Remember that you are the best solution for your fans
- Remember the problems you are solving for your fans
- Don't worry about losing people based on price – the right people will pay the right price. Price is merely a filter.
- Don't be cheap
- Remember that you can add different products into your product suite at different price points to enable you to help more people. A rule of thumb – the more of you that they get within the product the more expensive the product is within your suite.

Targets

Targets are really important. Targets can help you to stay motivated when you are feeling a little weary. They can drive you on further and faster when your energy for it feels low.

I can't even begin to count how many times I have been approaching the end of the month and realised that I am not a million miles away from hitting the target I put in place at the beginning of the month and that will drive me to continue to push forwards.

It's kinda like daring myself to be more, do more and serve more.

I can tell you now, if you're going to be all woolly about it all and vague then you might as well not bother.

Your goals and targets need to be specific, detailed and non-negotiable. When something is non-negotiable then you'll get it done.

Goals will give you the overarching motivator and your targets will help you to track your progress in order to get there.

You MUST write down your goals and targets. This will bring about a massive shift in itself. Apparently you are 42% more likely to achieve goals that are written down.

Work on them regularly.

Review them regularly.

I have targets for social media followers, income and list size. I tend to work with 3 big goals per month. One is always Income, one always List size and then I choose my SM of focus for the month.

Targets should be realistic but stretching.

The first thing that you need to do is to work out how much

you would like to earn in the next 12 months – what's your big figure? Divide that figure out through the months of the year, does that now look possible? It might be stretching but does it look possible?

What could you do/sell in order to achieve that level of monthly income?

Grab the free targets class in the resources accompanying this book >> www.beabusinessrockstar.com

Tracking

That which gets tracks invariably grows.

If you are not tracking your numbers now then take this as a sign to start – a copy of the numbers tracker that I use is available now in the resources area which accompanies this book, access it here >>> www.beabusinessrockstar.com

If you are not tracking your numbers then how do you know if you are hitting your targets?

If you don't track your income how do you know if you are hitting your targets? If you are popping your head deep into the sand then you may well end up with big problems biting you on the bottom. Knowledge is most definitely power.

Action Plan for Targets and Tracking

- Get a grip on where you are right now- ballpark/back of a fag packet calculations don't cut it
- Get your accounts up to date

- Do your accounts and other numbers monthly
- Track your income
- Start to sure up your income in advance – I enter each month with at least 75% of my income already sured up for that month through payment plans, instalments and ongoing projects.
- Stop fretting – it won't make any difference. Panicking, denial, avoidance, guilt, shame – all of those things won't change your position (all they do is drain you of your energy resources) but working towards your targets will.

CHAPTER REMINDER CHECKLIST

Remember...

Money is fantastic – it's not icky at all.

Make sure your sales pages and copy are fit for purpose and bring in results.

Pricing is about confidence, so DON'T be cheap.

Make your targets achievable but not too easy that they don't stretch you.

Keep on tracking, Rockstar.

11 HOW TO BUILD A ROCKSTAR TEAM

As they say, no man is an island. You won't build a BIG business is you run it like a toddler! How does a toddler run their business – I do it all BY MYSELF!!

It's impossible for you to be all things within your business in the long term.

When you first start out then you are all things, you wear a multitude of hats. You are the Accounts Manager, the Customer Services Officer, the PR Manager, the Admin Assistant, the Tech Support, the Coach, the Research Officer, the Marketing Manager blah blah blah (you get the picture) BUT there comes a time when you need to start to prioritise where your time is spent.

Starting to bring a team around you can be REALLY scary. It can feel like you are handing your baby out there for a complete stranger to take care of. You can feel like you are leaving yourself vulnerable. The biggest excuse, once people are financially able to get people on board with their team, is that it would take them longer to show someone how to do something rather than just getting on and doing it themselves. This is incredibly

181

short-sighted in a number of ways. Firstly, who's to say that that person wouldn't already know how to do that thing you want them to do. Secondly, who says you are doing it in the most efficient way. Thirdly – if you keep doing that thing it's going to cost you MILES more time than it would to show someone how to do it – NOT A VALID EXCUSE I'M AFRAID.

Investing a little bit of time in training people to assist you and in the ways that you like things to be done is absolutely priceless in the long run!

Just as a quick side note – You don't have to take on employees and everything that goes into employing people if you want to build a Rockstar Team. My whole team is outsourced, self-employed assistance to run my business.

It's taken me a little while to get a Rockstar Team around me and I have had some massive learning points along the way.

I have had some outsourcing disasters and some massive success.

Building a team round you to help and support you will help you to avoid the dreaded BURN OUT.

It will ensure that the ship can run smoothly when you're not around and it stops you doing the stuff that you ain't good at.

It can also help you to craft a bit of a "man down" system which means that if (for any reason) you can't be in your business at a given point in time then you can sound the Claxton and a system can rev into place that will mean that things still happen even when you aren't at the coal face of your business.

Before we talk about top tips for building a Rockstar Team let's talk about when outsourcing goes bad.

There have been occasions where I've been completely let down by my outsourced help. I had a lady who was helping me with admin and general day to day stuff within my business. One day, like a bolt out of the blue, I received an email from her that said that her intention was to cease trading with immediate effect. This lady was not only doing work for me but also for some of my Business Management VIP clients.

That support disappeared overnight and effectively trebled my workload.

The impact of this was that I ended up in a very stressful situation of picking up stuff and having to just get it done because there were no options available to me.

It was VERY stressful.

I survived though, and in a way, I'm quite lucky because everything that she did for us was stuff that I (predominantly) knew how to do.

The moral of the story was basically to make sure that you have a backup plan, either make sure that you know how things work within your business so that if you are ever in that situation you can pick things back up and get on with it. Or have a backup plan of someone else who can help you in case of sickness, illness or lost support.

My support team currently comprises of:

- Admin Support
- Photographer
- Graphic Designer
- Website Support & Design
- Accountant
- Social Media strategic support

My top tips for bringing together a Rockstar Team are...

Be careful with the whole peanuts and monkeys thing. You don't necessarily want to go with the cheapest prices. You would rather pay more per hour for someone who was more effective than less per hour for someone who will take forever to do something. You also need to be mindful about the quality of work.

You need to work with people who you can have a good working relationship with. My whole team I would now consider to be friends as well as colleagues. You need to be able to get on with your team.

Think about the jobs that you can outsource. You need to get clear on the things in your business that YOU need to do and the things that other people can help and support you with as well as outsourcing the stuff that you HATE doing too.

Be clear on expectations when engaging outsourced help. Make sure you are clear in which jobs you want them to complete, expected levels of support, turnaround times etc.

Make sure you are able to meet/speak with your outsourced team regularly. You need to keep in touch.

Make sure your outsourced team are aware of your business objectives.

Treat them well and they will look after you in return.

They can't read your mind. Communication is key. So many people get upset that things haven't been done properly BUT it's often the case that things just haven't been effectively communicated.

CHAPTER REMINDER CHECKLIST

Remember...

If you don't delegate you're going to burn yourself out.

Finding your team might take time but it's definitely worth it in the long-term.

Always have a back-up plan and know how to do any (or most) of the tasks you're outsourcing.

Value your team and they'll always have your best interests at heart too.

12 ROCKSTAR BUSINESS HACKS

Set aside slots of Cave Time, they don't need to be long.

Try CAVE time – one that I brought over from my corporate days. Known as Prime Time in my corporate days it's been adapted into cave time as I love to retreat into my cave and it is a totally awesome addition to my working structure. This is about dedicating periods of time to crack on with your work. It's about turning off all of the distractions and letting yourself get absorbed in the task at hand. I know what it's like when you are trying to get stuff done. You are working away and then a Facebook notification pops through or an email and you dizzy off to feed the notification noise. Boom – you're distracted, no coming back now. You've lost your rhythm and your mojo.

Is It Time?

Start before you are ready. Your ducks will never be in a row and there'll never be a perfect time (accept the perfect time is right now). Do that thing, take that step, make that leap.

Start as soon as you possibly can. I get that there's probably going to be a little bit of an internal battle that starts around the issue that goes a little something like this:

187

- I can do that work so I don't need to pay anyone else to do it.
- It will take longer for me to explain what needs to be done than just cracking on and doing it.
- I will have to wait if someone else is doing it.
- I need to have masses of input into it so I should just do it myself.
- I'm a control freak and no-one else will do it as well as me.

Yup, I've said all of those to myself. Guess what? They are **big fat lies.** Yes, there will be some stuff in your business that you have to do yourself. I look at the tasks that are mine and they revolve around writing, recording materials and service **– everything else has the ability to be outsourced.** It might take you a little longer on the first occasion to explain what you want doing but you will save stacks of time in the long run because your team member will be able to crack on and do it.

Waiting for someone else to do the tasks for you – it's about having an understanding, being clear on expectations/ deadlines etc but it means that you will start to think ahead a little more and stop being so reactionary. Plus... you know when you say "no-one else can do it as well as me"? That's your ego talking.

I started outsourcing before I was paying myself a salary.

Don't be a slave to the notification

I know that this one is totally counter intuitive. You wanna totally look after your fans, right?! Surely you need to be there for them in a flash? We are bombarded by notifications. Social Media pings, email whistles and life can feel like one long notification designed to grab your attention.

If you don't answer that Facebook notification or email for a couple of hours a day and few times per week it isn't going to be the end of the world.

Nothing bad will happen – I pinky promise!

Not only will it allow you to implement some cave time but it's good for boundaries too!

What Matters?

Your crowd needs to be central to all that you do.

Be an EXPERT

Lots of my lovely ladies shy away from this word. The word often brings out wobbles. Who do I think I am to say I'm an expert? I'm not REALLY an expert. You must claim it, live it, be it. If you don't then you aren't going to be a Rockstar.

This isn't one that's designed to make you feel wobbly but it's for you to look to step into your business and stop playing small.

Your crowd are looking to you to be a leader – go lead!

Who is your WHO?

Who are you marketing to? Now stop being wishy washy with this one. You need to get specific – but not in the ideal client kinda way, you need to be specific as to their commonality rather than their specificity!

Who are you serving, who are your fans?

We've talked about raving fans and there's more resources to help you with this one over in the resources attached to this book >> www.beabusinessrockstar.com

Stop hedging your bets, stop vomiting information out there without any clue of who you are talking to. Now IS the time to really work out who your fans are.

What do they need?

Working out what your crowd want/need from you, what they struggle with, and the problems you solve for them is the key that unlocks EVERYTHING.

Simples?

Simple BUT Significant is a mantra I love to work to.

Stop overcomplicating. Stop overthinking.
It doesn't have to be hard to be worth it.
Always, always, always keep it simple but significant.

Playing It Safe Will Keep You Small

Like I've said before in this book if you stop moving forwards, you stop growing. There's loads of clichés about how everything that you want is just on the other side of your comfort zone. We can talk about being brave until the cows come home BUT what you need to do is stretch and grow. That thing that frightens you the most is probably the thing that is most likely to bring you lots of change. Fear isn't a bad thing, what's important is that you can harness it and continue to move through it – even if you're just shuffling.

Flying Solo?

No one can do it for you but you can't do it all by yourself. Make sure you surround yourself with people who lift you higher, ask questions, and think about building a team around you to support you and your business.

Rockstar Team Building

Outsource the stuff you aren't good at or that takes you too much time. Starting to bring together a team is a FANTASTIC thing to do in your business. Outsourcing always seems to be the holy grail of business development. I often hear people say that they will be happy once they can bring a team around them and start getting that stuff off their desk – the stuff that causes them a massive headache.

I'm often asked if there's a point at which you should start to outsource, is there a magic time/place where a claxon sounds and marks the starting point of outsourcing?

I am also told that people don't outsource because they don't know what to outsource, how to get started and how to find help.

Are You Guilty

We are all guilty of 3 things (to varying degrees and at different times):

- standing in our own way
- overcomplicating stuff
- and taking the stuff we know for granted.

So... get out of your own way. You are your biggest barrier to success. Make sure you are sidestepping you, get help where you need it and keep moving forwards.

And... always look for the simplest and easiest solution to any problems or quandaries. Our natural inclination is to look for complicated answers and 99% of the time the simple solution is the best.

And remember... other people don't necessarily know the stuff that you know. Ditch the jargon, explain things (it's not patronising if you make sure you frame it in the right way) and be there for people to ask questions of you.

Every time You Think It's A Flop A Fairy Dies!

Tee hee hee. Okay, if you persuade yourself that something is going to flop then it will. I could get all woo wooo about this, we could talk about intention, alignment, law of attraction and much more BUT to make it super simple - if you start to put things out there with the wrong energy behind them then it will show.

If you set out marketing a programme with the thoughts of what you will do if no-one buys, then you are hardly setting yourself up for success. You need to commit to that programme or that freebie or whatever it is you're putting out there and you need to get yourself behind it 100%. None of this - what if it doesn't work guff - okay?

SERVE THE PANTS OFF YOUR CROWD

I'm a massive advocate of leading with service.

When you serve the pants off your crowd everything else follows.

It's also GREAT for getting over overwhelm, fear and frustration – just to serve the pants off them.

What can you do today to serve your crowd?

Here's some ideas;

- share something motivational or inspirational
- give them some top tips like these
- offer a free resource
- invite their questions and go answer them
- share your best blog
- write or record something that you know will get them unstuck
- ask them how you can help them even more.

Look after your crowd and everything will work out.

What Can I Do Today To Build My List?

One of the most important questions to ask yourself every day. That and, 'what can I do today to serve my fans?'

Your list is one of the few platforms where you gather your fans together that is under your control. It's the place you can contact your audience directly and drop into their inbox on your terms. It's also where you can nurture more relationships, give more help and assistance and be there for your fans. List building is SO important. Write it on a post it note and stick it to your desk – What Can I Do Today To Build My List?

What can I Sell You For Free?

This one ties in with the last once nicely. It is all about the fantastic freebie. What can you give to your crowd in exchange for their email address? When you first start out it's scary giving stuff away for free. You feel like you are give give giving BUT that's fine, that's exactly what you should be doing. You should be positioning yourself as the expert, giving away more than is comfortable and letting your audience sample your AWESOMENESS without having to pull out their credit cards.

Testimonials make a Rockstar

NEVER underestimate the power of social proof. Social proof is AWESOME. People know you are going to say that your stuff is amazing. People know what marketing speak is all about. They don't expect you to come out and say "fancy joining my mediocre programme?" Testimonials bring a whole new level of proof that what you do works. Your raving fans will be more than willing to write you testimonials because you have changed their world. When you are a Rockstar your fans will appreciate what you do for them and will be willing to share that with others.

Check Out Your "About Me" Page

It's one of the most neglected website pages BUT one of the most viewed by people. Who are you? People want to delve in a little deeper and find out a little bit more about you. Don't neglect it. Make sure that you update it, keep it fresh and relevant and actually use that space well. Take a look around internetty land for some examples of how people are using their About Me page for some inspiration. This is your chance to let your fans get to know you and for you to blow your trumpet a little.

What's Your Big Promise?

What will I achieve by working with you? What's your promise? What is the end result? Obviously you can't guarantee that everyone will achieve the end result because they need to take on board your advice and teachings and implement them. I know the results that my clients get if they work through exactly what I teach and implement it. Those who embrace the programmes get AMAZING results.

Voice Record Your Sales Page and Capture The Passion

It's REALLY hard to get your passion into words sometimes. You edit yourself too much, you apply too many filters, you lose the essence of what you're trying to say. My BIGGEST piece of advice here is to voice record your sales pages before you type them up. This way you are less likely to filter yourself, you get MUCH more passionate about your programmes when you talk about them and you will capture that passion. You can then type up the results and edit as applicable.

What Does Your Website Say About You?

Don't have an amateur website. Make sure your website conveys who you are and your message. Make sure it's in alignment with your business and brand. I know that websites can be a royal old pain in the ass BUT if you do this on the cheap it'll show. I spent a considerable period of time doing my own websites. I am capable but they aren't all that beautiful. I need my website to be a Sales Person on my team, I need it to be Customer Relations, Sales, Contact, Source of Value, Shop Window all in one.

Take a Look at your Timeline

One that we so often forget. I was talking to a lovely lady the other day and she said that it was one of the greatest take homes she had had about her social media marketing. Periodically have a scoot down your social media page.

- Can I tell what it is that you do?
- What you are all about?
- Is it easy to find out how to contact you or find out more,
- Is your about section up to date,
- Are there links back to your website?

Focus on the important stuff

It's so easy to get bogged down in the day to day stuff of running your business. It's easy to try to do everything yourself and end up achieving nothing. You may well think you can do everything but the chances are that if you try to do everything nothing will get done properly. If it doesn't involve creating content or building relationships with your audience or driving sales then you must question whether IT needs doing and if IT does whether it should be outsourced.

Ask – what's it bringing to the party (if it ain't rocking up with a bottle or some nibbles then it can leave).

Following on from the tip above this is what I ask myself – what does it bring to the party? You could ask this about most things in your business and if you are doing it because you just got stuck in a rut then now's the time to stop it. If it does bring something to the party but doesn't need doing by you then you need to look to outsource it.

Don't reinvent the bloomin wheel

We discussed this one in the marketing chapter and it's important that you don't spend your life trying to reinvent the wheel. It's exhausting and unnecessary. Remember to look at how many ways you can use each piece of content within your business and how you can leverage your time.

Rockstars don't make things overly complicated.

Simple is always better.

The mantra is always – Simple BUT Significant.

Be authentic & have integrity

Two of your biggest assets in your business. Being authentic is about you being you. No-one else can be you and this is the way that you will start to make sure that your business becomes copy proof. Secondly, your authenticity will let you stand out. It's not complicated, it's about you being you. Your integrity allows the TRUST factor of the "know, like and trust" calculation to grow. Your crowd need you to be trustworthy. They need you to be working with the highest integrity and they don't want to have to question your motives in business.

A quick word of warning – the thing iabout being authentic is that you don't have to tell anyone you are doing it!!

Lots of people flag things up as being "authentic" and are often use the word as an apology for things not being super slick or polished. It's ok not to be super slick or polished – you don't need to apologise for it.

People know whether or not you're being authentic – permission not to have to flag it up or feel that you have to try to prove it.

Just be yourself – real, raw & nothing more

Tell a Tale

Marketing is all about storytelling. It's all about painting a picture and allowing people to get absorbed in what you have to say. You should be telling the story of you and how you came to be doing what you do. People will love to hear your back story because, by nature, we are all REALLY nosey. You should also be telling stories within your content. It brings things to life. Not only does it make your stuff easier to read and understand (less dull and boring) but it also allows you to continue to infuse your personality in all that you do.

Take Your Time

It's a marathon and not a sprint – yada yada yada BUT it's even more than that. When you rush stuff you'll make mistakes. If you are constantly sprinting along then you will make bad decisions. I'm all for sprinting when necessary and when the situation demands it but on a day to day basis you need to make sure you aren't making mistakes, you aren't just vomiting stuff out there in a hurry and that you are being strategic in what you do.

Videos Rock

Videos are great for Rockstars. People love to be able to put faces and voices to your brand. People will connect with you more easily and deeply if they are watching your videos and they will feel like they know you more. Videos don't always need to be fully produced and expensive – although there is a place for some produced videos in your business and on your website.

Don't do the stuff you're pants at

This is the story of delegation. So many people struggle with the stuff that they ain't good at. They will spend hours, no actually – days, trying to master a certain piece of tech. The thing is that at the outset they will say that they can't afford to outsource it BUT the reality is that they can't afford not to. When you are wasting hours of your life trying to do things that you aren't good at then you aren't immersing yourself in income generating activities. When you waste time you make less money. You're NOT doing anything to grow your business whilst you are wrestling with that particular thing. If you don't NEED to learn how to do it then outsource it. AND before you panic, it's not going to take an expert in that field the same amount of time to mess about with as it took you. Often, that thing that you have been struggling with for hours (or even days and weeks), will take a Virtual Assistant/Webby Person/Graphic Designer 20 minutes and therefore won't be as expensive as you think.

Take Time Off

This one took me a while to grasp. I thought that the only way that I could be a success was if I worked harder and faster than everyone else. If I was constantly head down and pushing forwards then I would win the race. Alas, I was feeding myself lies!! It's just as important to rest as it is to work.

If you don't take time off then you don't see the bigger picture. If you are constantly working then you make bad decisions. If you don't take your time then you make mistakes.

Time off is as important as your work time. It's the time when you can let your creativity re-charge, you will get some fantastic new ideas when your mind is free to roam and you'll be much more enthusiastic about your business in the long term.

Overnight success takes a long time

Overnight success takes longer than overnight – FACT (sorry). Yes, there are times when Coaches seem to appear out of thin air and become REALLY successful but in every circumstance I have seen of this happening it's taken them a long time to get there AND there is a backstory to their business and success. It takes longer than you think to build a tribe. It's about being consistent, it's about being there for them and it's about serving the pants off them.

Track Your Money

Stop avoiding it, stop burying your head in the sand. You need to know your numbers. You need to how much you are bringing in, the level of income you have guaranteed for the weeks/months ahead, how much you need in order to cover your expenses and pay yourself. It's time to start to track your money, anally if necessary. That which is tracked grows, that which is watched can be turned around. Disasters can be diverted and growth can be sought. Ignorance isn't bliss, ignorance will get you into A LOT of trouble.

Aim For The Target

Add targets into your business. Targets will help you monitor how things are going and will often encourage you to take that additional step in your quest to achieve them. BUT don't become number centric as that will result in your business losing its soul.

Nosey Bitch

Be an observer of EVERYTHING! Watch for the content which catches your eye. Ask yourself – what is it that made me stop and look at this? It might be the emails you open in your inbox – why do you open certain ones immediately and not others? It might be that Facebook post that stopped you flicking through your newsfeed – what made you stop? It might be that blog that you were compelled to read – why? The more you observe the things that you like, the more inspiration you will have to create compelling content in your business.

Top tip – look at the stuff that you don't like too! I subscribe to

201

certain emails because I don't like them, I would have normally hit unsubscribe immediately but I let them continue to fall into my inbox so that I can keep a check on why I don't like them and make sure I'm not doing those things in my business.

Live your brand

You are your brand and you need to be comfortable living your brand. Your brand needs to ooze you and you need to ooze your brand.

You need to make sure that everything fits together, that everything you do within your business is a perfect match to your brand. You need to find your style and stick with it.

Don't lose the crowd connection

Don't disconnect yourself with your crowd. Don't move away from keeping your ear to the crowd and be driven by serving your fans.

If you disconnect from your crowd, stop listening, become a little too aloof (I'm not saying that you should be easily accessible to all of your crowd BUT you do need to keep them at the forefront of your mind), disconnection disconnects.

Be a leader

You are the leader of your fans, you are the leader in your business, you are the BEST fit for your fans. You are the person who is going to help them to get unstuck.

Act like a bloomin leader, stop hiding, stop being cheap – just stop it already. It's time to stand up as the leader of your brand and be a Rockstar.

Keep Your Eyes Open

Be mindful of the levels of engagement from your crowd. Keep an eye on the things they are responding to. Are there certain types of posts they are responding to on your social media platforms, or certain blogs that are getting more eyes on them than others, or certain e-newsletters that are achieving a better click through rate? What does this tell you about the types of content/help your audience want to consume?

Perfect Or Pants?

Don't wait for stuff to be perfect.

Remember that things which are stuck in your perfection filters cannot help anyone. It's really normal to get stuck in a quest for perfection BUT this will keep you stuck.

Seeking perfection might be about keeping yourself safe, it might be about not putting that thing out there, it might be wrapped up in self-confidence/esteem issues BUT it's time to sidestep that one a little.

You are responsible for taking action in your business. No-one else can do this stuff for you. You have to do the stuff. Don't get stuck in over-planning, don't get stuck in learning and not implementing, don't get stuck waiting for perfection. Take the action and do the stuff you need to do.

It might scare the pants off you at first. Business isn't about being fearless. It's about knowing that the fear isn't greater than your mission, and accepting and embracing that the fear is a sign that you are about to do something to help you grow and evolve.

Where are you leaving cash behind?

Are you stifling your income by not being able to see the obvious – remember the "just because I could doesn't mean I should" mantra here BUT are there really obvious ways where you are not making the most of your income or holes in your expenditure that mean you have money leaks?

Know what your crowd want

If you don't know the answer to this one then you need to ask them. What your crowd WANT is what they will take out their cash for.

There's no MAGIC formula

As I scroll through my newsfeed today I see that I am being promised the #1 technique/secret/ ninja results formula to double my business or quadruple my list, have a six figure launch (regardless of my biz or whether I have a crowd) or be able to work 2 hours once a fortnight and be a trillionaire blah blah blah!!Ok, there is no secret formula, no magic one size fits all checklist for growing your business. You will need to put the work in. It won't just fall on your lap. It's about looking at your business as a whole and taking marketing techniques which fit your business, you and your crowd perfectly. No unrealistic promises, no liar liar pants on fire. There are things you need to be doing and things you definitely shouldn't be doing BUT this is not a magic spell out of Hogwarts that only a few people are allowed to know. Time for me (and you) to sieve out the rubbish!

Focus on the goals – why are you doing it?

Why do you do what you do? What is your BIG goal(s)? In the past I found it really difficult to quantify what I wanted my life to look like, what I was working towards. I couldn't manage a vision board for the life of me. I just couldn't do it. I had no idea what I wanted. If you don't know what you want and how you want your business to look how can you quantify success? How will you know when you have "made it?" What will you do to keep yourself motivated when you are having a slog period? It's important that you dream (visualise the ultimate goal) and that you know what you want your business to look like and what you want your life to look like as a result of your business.

Respect your workspace

You need space to be creative but that's not just about having time to get down and write your blogs and content but you need an area where you work that you love. A happy place. A place that inspires you. It needs to be a place that's just for your work and that doesn't feel like you have to pack away your business every time you finish working. I have an office at home and an office away from home as well as working in other locations when I fancy a change of scenery. I'm blessed that I can work from anywhere but I also like to have a little space where me & my business are "at home".

Guard your work time

Your work time is important. Just because you work from home it doesn't mean that you are available to take delivery of everyone's parcels or that people can just pop round for a coffee whenever they feel like it. Your work time is important. Developing your business is important. Yes, it's awesome that when you're a Rockstar that you can be flexible with your time BUT it's also important that that flexibility doesn't result in you leaking time and not getting stuff done. You can't grow your business without investing time in that growth.

Everything needs a reason

Why are you doing it? It's often a question I ask my lovely clients. It's one that often makes them stop dead in their tracks. So why are you doing that? Urm, not sure?! Everything you do needs to fit into the big plan, it needs to have a reason and you need to know that it's either establishing or nurturing relationships, adding value or is income generating. If it's not one of those things WHY are you doing it?

Content is your biz

Content is the cornerstone of any online business. Whether it's your free content or your programme content. Make sure you aren't cutting corners with your content. Make sure you are protecting your content. Make sure you are showing your content in the very best light. Be proud of what you create.

Every piece of content has a gazillion uses. Don't think that because it's been posted once, it's been done. Remember, every idea can be a text post, an image, a video, a blog, a podcast and then you can recycle it and use it again. You don't have to be constantly in creation mode.

Content is king. Captivate and inspire your crowd through your content and give without expectation. Serve the pants off your crowd in all you do.

Over-deliver

Over-deliver, make people feel well looked after in all you do.

You Need To Be A Sat Nav

Think of yourself as a bit of a Sally Sat Nav for your crowd. You are guiding the way. YUP, potentially they could take this journey alone but there's every possibility that they would get lost, take a detour or even loop back to where they started. Think about the journey you'll take them on and plot the route. You are going to take them straight to their destination and stop them from getting distracted or sidetracked.

Where are you not being a pro?

Check out where you are being cheap. Where are you avoiding spending money despite the fact that you know, deep down, that an investment needs to be made? Where are you just cobbling things together and hoping for the best because you aren't spending the right amount of time on it? Where are you vomiting stuff out there without much thought? Would (insert whoever it is that you look up to within business) do that? You will then get your answer!

Social Media Vortex

Unless your job is social media then your job isn't social media. Lots of people get distracted and sucked into the social media vortex. Yes, social media is an A-MAZING place to gather your crowd, to build a community and to gain traction and visibility BUT, be there with a purpose and avoid its distracting, attention-seeking behaviours.

Have You Collected All The Eggs?

Make sure you don't put all your eggs in one basket. Build a social media platform but also look to bring your followers over to being subscribers and send out newsletters that nourish their soul.

Get Ya Pom-poms Out

Be a cheerleader for your crowd. Help and support them, be there for them, answer their questions, love them hard and serve the pants off them.

Find yourself some cheerleaders too.

There are 2 ways you need to look at this one.
1. Some of your best cheerleaders will be happy customers/clients. They are like your little unpaid sales force who will spread the word about what you do. Encourage people to spread that word. So often now we are asked to leave reviews on Facebook pages/Trip Advisor and the likes – are you encouraging that? Are you encouraging people to recommend you to people they know?

2. We are not all on top form all of the time, and having a group of cheerleaders around you that will help pick you up on a pants day, who will celebrate your successes with you and kick your butt when necessary is PERFECT to help you evolve and get out of your own way.

Chin Chin

Celebrate your successes. We are all very quick to pick on what we haven't done and beat ourselves because we aren't where we want to be, BUT you must give yourself credit for how far you've come and celebrate the wins (even the little ones).

Loose The Amnesia

Remember how far you've come. Yes, don't be distracted by looking back (coz you're not going that way!) BUT give yourself a big old high five for how much you've learned, grown and developed.

Let The Cashflow Flow

Cashflow is the lifeblood and oxygen in your business. Without money coming in your business will soon stagnate. It's important that you don't avoid looking at the numbers. If you avoid looking at the numbers then the numbers will bite you on the butt. You will either get to the end of the year and realise that you don't make any money OR you will get to the end of the year and find out that you made more money than you anticipated and have a tax liability as a result.

Working On Purpose

Before I had kids I was a bit of a Monica (think **Friends,** think control freak). I totally chilled out on this one when I realised that actually, things usually work out in the end. BUT, having a to-do list is SUPER good for your business. A long to-do list mustn't overwhelm you – in fact it's a good thing because it means that there are stacks of action steps you can take in order to develop your business. Downloading all you need to do into a list will mean that your brain is set free of trying to remember everything and will allow your mental capacity to actually take action.

Do You Need A Plunger?

It's your responsibility to remove the blocks that you are putting in your own way. The self- talk fairy will try to batter you with all the reasons why you can't do that particular thing. I have a two-pronged attack to this bad boy.

1. Write down what's coming up on the self-talk front – the minute that you write it down you discharge it of its power – then play a little game of truth or lie. Is that point the truth or is it a big fat lie?
2. The Evidence Base – bring together a notebook which is your evidence base about what a good job you do. You might spend some time writing in it when you have just finished a project and are really excited about what you've achieved, or when a client has had a massive breakthrough, or when you have got some lovely feedback or a testimonial. Refer back to your evidence base whenever you are feeling a little wobbly.

Innovate

Innovate, try new things – stagnant smells and it's always a good idea to try out something new and exciting. It won't always be a roaring success but you will only ever fail if you stop trying.

Investments need to be made — don't try and do it on the cheap

I have worked with lots of ladies who are PETRIFIED of making the next investment in their business. I have been there. I know what it's like. When I first started in business I spent more money on learning all about business and marketing than I paid myself. I paid my coach more than I paid myself. I sometimes had to bite the bullet and purchase a particular piece of software or a certain tool. It's uncomfortable at first BUT if you need it to develop your business then you need to find a way to make that purchase. It's only going to keep you small if you don't make that call. You will waste time and stifle your growth and income if you don't.

Why Plan?

This might sound like it's an obvious one "well you plan so that you know what you're doing". BUT it's so much more than that. You plan in order to see whether your targets are realistic. You plan because it's important for you to have an element of structure to what you are doing so that you don't end up confusing your crowd. You plan because it helps you to make good decisions.

Don't sell your soul

Becoming a Rockstar is definitely not about selling your soul to the devil. **DO NOT DO THINGS THAT DON'T SIT RIGHT WITH YOU ETHICALLY.** If it feels a bit icky then chances are that it is. Remember this is your business and you can do it your way (as long as you keep sidestepping yourself & avoid getting in your way).

Copy Cat

So I know that it's a common one and it's one that leaves you feeling a little bit anxious, out of whack and downright pissed off!

Copying!! It's totally ok!

I know that I see lots of my words and phrases and teachings being used by others. It's kinda like being a stock image – if you put yourself out there then chances are that you will see yourself out there in the world.

It's kinda a twofold thing.

If you are teaching other people and helping and supporting them in their growth then you would be naive to think that people wouldn't take what you're telling them and pass it on. You are providing them with the teaching and inspiration. I would never suggest that people copy others because copying is lame. It's about bringing things forth with your own life lens and your own personality and doing it your way – you can't be me (and to be honest, you probably wouldn't want to be – tee hee hee). You need to be the best version of you and do stuff your way. It's about you entering into your 2.0 version of yourself.

If you teach and support others then the ripple effect dictates that they spread that on and if there's an element of you in there then that's ok.

These people will find their own way. Sometimes it's simply bystanders who seek to copy your awesome. Let me just tell you that success leaves clues but never tells a full story.

SO WHAT IF SOMEONE TOTALLY OVERSTEPS THE MARK?

I know that lots of people have circumstances whereby they feel that someone is being a little bit disrespectful or they are simply overstepping the mark. It might be something they say, might be something they do or it might be a social media post.

I see it most often when people are hosting Facebook groups and other people think it's ok to pop in and advertise the same service as the host provides to their crowd, #notok!
BUT it can happen in loads of other ways too (like overly zealous use of inspirations, unsolicited "feedback" to name just a few).

So, what can you do about it?

- Step back, I know that it's difficult to believe whilst you are in the emotion of it but there are times where people don't know it would cause an issue. Chances are they would be mortified about the fact that they had upset you or overstepped the mark.
- If it upsets you then address it because there's nothing good going to come from holding on to that angst. Contacting someone out of the blue about these kinda things needs thinking through. Don't do it whilst you are feeling all uptight about it and make that first contact unpleasant by jumping in all accusing and derogatory, this will only get other people's hackles up.
- If that initial contact bears no fruit then look at your options, get a little advice and consider things objectively. Try to take the emotional charge out of it as far as you can.
- Deal with it in the best energy, without kneejerk reactions and know that most of the time people don't mean to upset you, be mean or overstep anything.

213

What Should You Sell?

Sell products that fit your crowd perfectly. Take some time to think about what they WANT. People are much more willing to whip out their purses for things that they WANT rather than things that they NEED. You sell them what they WANT and give them what they NEED in order to achieve the desired WANT.

Change It Up Sister

If stuff isn't working then change it. You need to make sure you aren't impatiently changing things without giving them a chance to get traction. But it's in your hands to tweak and change elements that don't feel right or aren't getting the results you'd like.

Stop Wasting Opportunities

I have a feeling that you are sometimes doing this.

You are wasting opportunities.

I know you don't mean it, I know that it just kinda happens.

A lot of the time it's about selling. You just can't get it quite right, you panic and you vomit some information out there just to fill the void. It's better to post something than nothing, right?

Perhaps you are simply being a little too polite with your marketing and perhaps you are simply waiting for your sales page to do all of the work for you, and you aren't paying any attention to the means by which you are seeking to drive the traffic there.

It's your DUTY to help the people that you are here to help. It's up to you to show them the awesomeness that they could get their hands on and that it's all just a click away. Whether it's products, programmes, services etc you need to be telling the world about them. People can't buy from you if they know nothing about what you do.
So let's take a look....

** Being Too Polite**

I also look at it as stealth marketing. This is where you are alluding to something you have for sale but you are simply not telling anyone about it. You are looking to raise curiosity but then you fail to follow through. You are giving them a bit and leaving them questioning what it's all about.

Your crowd can't read your mind.

Your crowd need you to tell them about the products and services you offer and allow them to make a decision as to whether it's a good fit for them or not.

Don't leave them questioning what it's all about. People are busy, people want to make decisions as to whether they are prepared to invest more time in reading the sales page.

Vomiting Links

Just popping links into your social media marketing and saying that you have something available to buy is a waste of your marketing bandwidth.

You're not telling people anything.

215

You having something for sale isn't necessarily going to get them to take the time to make the click.

You need to give them a little bit more.

I would LOVE it if you optimised your marketing opportunities. Don't waste them and leave people wondering what's in it for them.

So, what do you need to do?

- Work out who your products and programmes are for and use that in your marketing.
- Tell them what's in it for them.
- Entice them with a little more information.

Hiding your selling in polite, stealth ways won't allow you to help the people you are here to help and simply vomiting links is also going to stop you from reaching as many people as you could.

Take those opportunities.

Take your time to get the marketing behind them right.
Shine your beacon bright so that the people who you are here to serve can be captivated by you and want to find out more.

Sometimes less is more and sometimes more is more but either way you need to let people know what's in it for them.

Are you hiding?

You might not even realise you are doing it. You might just be accepting the polite little bits, you might be using photographs of anything but you, you might be speaking very "professionally" in all that you do, you might be talking yourself out of ever taking a punt, a risk or being brave. Ask yourself regularly if you are hiding. It can creep up on you and bite you on the bum at any time.

Step Out From Behind The Brand

You must step out from behind your brand.

Stop hiding behind your computer and/or your branding. I know it's kinda like holding a cushion over your face during a scary movie – somehow it feels super safe BUT safe isn't always the best option!

They are stacks of businesses out there which I know (for certain) are run by amazing, strong women who are brimming full of personality but what they are doing in their business is just plain boring. The messages that they put out there are NOT inspiring, rallying or in any way reflecting the passion and drive they have for their business or their products & services.

They are selling themselves short.

They are being same old, same old.

They are blending into the background at best. And at worst they are just repelling people in the opposite direction.

It is tragic, they could be helping so many more people if they just allowed who they are & what they do to shine through.

It is so true that people buy from people. If people make a connection with you, form a relationship with you, grow to like you then they are going to trust you. They will trust what you say, they will see you as an expert, an authority if you will, & they will feel safer & more secure in buying from you. That, of course, is the ultimate aim of your marketing.

So it all boils down to the "know, like & trust" factor. People wanna get to know you, form that relationship, start to like you and then they will trust you.

Hiding away behind your brand or your computer, adding no personality to anything you do and not letting your audience know a little bit about you will result in less sales. Don't be afraid to come out from behind the branding, your ideal customer will LOVE you, LOVE how you are authentic and real with them, and LOVE getting to know you and becoming a customer.

So now is the time, strip off those vanilla shackles, stop being boring and let your audience get to know you a bit!

I know it'll feel a little uncomfortable at first but guess what, just like your jeans, when stuff's uncomfortable it means that you are growing!

Side-step Yourself

We often are the ones who get in our own way. We put boundaries in place, we have beliefs that we can't do certain things or deal with certain things in a certain way. We obstruct the path to success from ourselves. I suppose some people would call it self- sabotage but I see it more as the protector in your brain is standing in your way, it's keeping you safe, it's stopping you from getting hurt. It's full of self-talk about how scary the road to success is and why you need to protect yourself. It's kinda like that helicopter parent at the park who is hovering over the top of their child shouting "eeee be careful", "don't climb up there", "watch this/that/the other". Like a child who is growing up you just need to say – do you know what, I'm ok, I can do this, I know it seems a little scary but what's the worst that can happen?

Copy Proof

Your business becomes copyproof when you infuse it with you and your personality. Don't be afraid to shine within your business.

Do you need an alter ego?

Sometimes you won't feel very confident. Sometimes you will just want to hide and not let anyone in. That's normal! But you might need a business alter ego. Take on the persona and just keep going until your confidence returns. Hitch on your cape and get on with the task in hand.

Can I Ask You Something..

Ask your crowd questions – OFTEN. Questions are an AMAZING inclusion in your marketing mix for a number of reasons.

1. They are going to help you to find out what your crowd want – their interests etc.
2. It brings a sense of community to your social media platform.
3. Questions allow you to accelerate the know/like and trust factor with your crowd.

Make your questions easy to answer and easy for people to get involved with.

They don't have to be oh so serious and just about the work that you do. Ask your crowd questions that are more about their world or their likes and dislikes (this isn't frivolous interaction – this helps you to continue to develop the profile of your crowd and can ultimately help you when it comes to bringing together targeting for your advertising etc).

Whatever you do don't give up

The amount of clients I have had to cajole over the years to keep going is quite a large number. It might be that they are coming towards the end of a launch and they are exhausted, all they want to do is to stop now, they can't be bothered to close the doors on their launch, they are bored of talking about it. One Rockstar I cajoled into closing her doors with an official email to her list DOUBLED yes DOUBLED her numbers with that single email because all of a sudden people didn't want to miss out.

It's also often the case that our ego says to us that things aren't working as we would like and we are just going to give up, call it a day and hide under a rock. You never know who's watching, you never know who is poised to become your next customer. You never know what is just around the corner. You need to have the self-discipline and drive to keep going when your ego or your energy levels are telling you to stop BUT also the sense to know when things need tweaking because they aren't working. Giving up too early will just not work. It's often most obvious when people go to sell their first programmes and they don't get people falling over themselves to buy immediately. They then panic and hide – that won't help you build relationships and move through to selling things to your fans.

Make stuff happen

Dreaming or doing? Doing every time. You can't just dream

about the day you have this big business. It's all about thinking the right way and doing the right things. Progress loves action. Without action progress is never going to happen. Crack on lovely!

Stock Take

Take stock of your stock – obviously if you are a product-based business then you will already keep an eye on your stock. If you are a digital business then this sometimes goes by the wayside. Take a look at what you've got right now and what you could sell to your crowd.

Do you heart marmite? (you should)

I'm not saying that you have to like the taste of the vile dark substance (bork – can you tell which camp I'm in there?) But you can't be all things to all people. Being a Rockstar is not a popularity contest. It's about you attracting the RIGHT people, speaking to the RIGHT people with your message.

Not everyone is going to love what you do. But, guess what, that's ok. Actually, that's more than ok, it's AWESOME.

You need to be attracting the people to your business who will become your fans, people who value you and what you do – not just anyone and everyone.

It's not ok to be inconsistent

There is one thing that it's not ok to be and that's inconsistent. Inconsistency is BAD. When you are inconsistent people just don't know where they stand with you. Your fans will enjoying seeing your updates, information and advice when you're on it BUT then they'll feel like you just disappear. Being consistent with your email newsletter, being consistent with your social media posts, being a consistent presence is elevating you and helping you serve your crowd.

Consistency is key. Consistency in message, consistency in showing up, consistency across platforms where people can find you, and consistency in introducing yourself and what you do. (Remember that people take different things from your message at different times so don't be afraid of repeating yourself.)

Don't Make It Hard

Make the buying process easy and efficient for your crowd. On sooooo many occasions I have looked a people's websites and found complicated and convcluted buying processes that include sending emails and making contact before being able to do business. Sometimes there are too many choices, and, worst of all, the payment/order buttons do not work.

Look at your purchase process through the eyes of your customer and see if there's any ways you can streamline it/make it easier.

Every day is a good day to be awesome

Even if yesterday was a SUPER bad day every day is a chance to start again. Every day is a chance for you to decide that it's your time. You don't have to wait until a Monday or a New Year to transform into a Rockstar – today is a very good day to do it.

Are you bloody overwhelming?

Gosh there are some people out there who are just so intense, confusing and overwhelming. Make sure that you know what your message is in everything that you do, lighten up and let your fans have a little bit of you AND remember what it's like to not know your specialist subject. Overwhelming your fans will make them zone out, they won't get you and therefore you will struggle to develop a relationship with them.

Are You Overwhelmed?

Overwhelm will keep you stuck.

Overwhelm is having lots of ideas and no idea where to start. Start by doing a braindump of everything that is coming up for you. Write it all down and set it free.

The best way to get started?? Start! Choose 5 jobs from your list and set about ticking them off.

When you bring together the list I advocate a realistic, action-based to-do list. This means you can take the action designated on the list, rather than having a task which says "sort out website" that could well be broken down into 50 smaller action points.

Tick things off the list (because it's cathartic).

A big to-do list means you have lots of actions that can help move your business forwards. If you get everything ticked off your to-do list, however, beware because it means your business has stagnated.

Avoid The Tech Tantrums

Software and technology soon becomes second nature. I know that technology can cause tantrums and terror in heart-centred entrepreneurs but we all start out not knowing. When I first started in business I didn't even have a personal social media account. I could only use Word and a legal specific case management system. I've invested time and effort in learning. I have acknowledged that it's all a step by step process and that you can get your hands in and fiddle and learn as you go.

Don't let tech have power over you – it's like children and animals and it can sense when you are scared!

Some Launch Love

Launch periods can be incredibly intensive. It's important that you build up to them by making sure you have prepared in advance as much as you possibly can. Make sure you are rested and your cup is overflowing and you are in good health. Think about the silly things like making sure you have healthy food in the house, you are drinking enough water, you are getting fresh air, and you are able to support yourself during your launch too. It easy to get caught up in it so make sure you plan ahead and do the necessary to take care of yourself during the launch period too. Launch periods can leave you feeling like a student – late nights, burning the candle at both ends, and making poor eating choices. Prepare in advance, batch cook, have good boundaries around your working hours and get plenty of water, fresh air and exercise. You won't get your best results if you are tired, ratty and depleted.

Constant Coalface = Dirty Face

Remember your way and don't get lost in constant busyness. It's important that you spend a little bit of time helicptering out of your business in order to get an objective view of the direction in which it's going. Being constantly at the coal face can result in you stalling and stagnating.

Lights, Camera....

If you are frightened of videos then I promise you that the first is always the worst.

Lots of people avoid doing videos because it scares the pants off them. I get it, I remember doing my first videos, and I also relive it with lots of my Rockstars when I Rockstar Dare them to get their first videos out there.

So, what are my top tips? Let's check them out.

- Have your camera at the right height. Don't look down at the camera because it makes you seem like you are looking down on your viewers. Want to avoid a jowly look? Sit your camera slightly higher and point it down > it talks lbs off you.
- Get your lighting right. It can be as simple as having a desk lamp shining towards your face, or investing in a cheap umbrella light from Amazon. I think mine cost about £20. You don't have to invest in anything fancy dan.
- The likelihood is that the camera and microphone on your computer is sufficient – again, you don't need to invest in any fancy dan equipment.
- Eyes on the camera rather than on yourself.
- Smile.
- Relax, yes I know it's easy to say ALTHOUGH it can be more difficult in real life. The trick to this one is just doing it a few times. Once you have done a few videos you will soon get over yourself and relax right into it. I find with lots of my Rockstars that the fear usually switches

225

into enjoying videos and finding them MUCH easier than writing.

- Think you'll forget what you are going to say? You can use a teleprompter app and have it on a tablet device beside you. Alternatively, you can pop the key points you want to cover on post-it notes and stick them on your screen to remind you of what you want to cover. I don't script my videos but if I have certain points that I want to cover I use the olde post-it note technique.
- Remember, you are judging yourself much more than anyone else ever would. If you don't do videos then you are robbing your crowd of the opportunity to get more help from you, you are not capitalising on your relationship building and you aren't utilising the opportunity to gain the fantastic reach that video can achieve. So it REALLY is time to get over yourself!
- If you are using videos on Facebook then don't use a YouTube link, always upload them directly into Facebook.
- Remember to add your videos to YouTube as it's the second largest search engine in the WORLD and you can then have your own little TV show.
- Leverage your videos. A single video can be uploaded to Facebook and YouTube and then shared on your website, on Pinterest, on Twitter and popped in your content library to use over and over again.
- Batch record your videos. For whatever reason (and I've never been accused of having OCD), I record in 5s. I will record 5 videos at a time, simply by changing my scarf, re-arranging my hair or changing my top - no-one would ever know.
- THE MOST IMPORTANT ONE >> be yourself, don't worry if you stumble on some words here and there, don't panic about chatting through things, just pretend you are having a chat with a member of your crowd.

I reckon that once you start doing them you will start to LOVE videos!

Mixed messages are confusing

As a follow on to the above, mixed messages are massively confusing. I often speak to people who have decided and (they say they have) committed to taking a certain path within their business BUT they continue to be hedging their bets as far as their message and crowd are concerned. They are sending mixed messages out there. They are not being clear in what it is that they do and they are confusing people. Make sure you aren't sending mixed messages out there.

Professional is relative

When I was a lawyer I had to be "professional" I had to write things in certain ways and I had to use a certain type of language. I run my business very professionally but I don't beat myself with a stick that says you need to be professional. I decided very early on in my business that I wanted to write the way I spoke, that I wanted to be the real me. I write in exactly the same way as I would if I was speaking to you over a cuppa. If we meet in "real life" you will get the same me as you get on the pages of this book. Perhaps I don't always write in the Queen's English, perhaps I upset the Grammar Police at times but, frankly, I don't care. My fans don't care either (ok, one or two of them are correcting the grammar in their heads but that's cool).

Always be open to possibility

My lovely friend & client Kate Spencer wrote the most fantastic books 1*2 Lessons* & *12 Lessons Later*. Lesson 1 was about being open to possibility and it's a lesson that I have tried to incorporate into my life always. You never know what's round the corner, you never know which opportunities may come to knock. Yes, at times you make your own opportunities, but never be closed to those which just come knocking. If you are closed to possibilities, then you are going to miss out MASSIVELY.

Love your list

List love is a MUST. The people who have invested their email address in you are a special bunch. They are people who have opted to hear from you. They have invested in continuing a relationship with you. Don't let them down. Don't constantly bombard them with sales emails and make them feel like walking purses. The people on your list are the people who are most likely to buy from you. They are your most invested fans behind your customers. They are into you! Respect them, take care of them, add value to them and look after them.

Keep The Crib

Keep a crib file. Whenever you are going through anything for the first time then make sure you keep a crib file. This will make it so much easier next time.

If you are learning a new process, keep notes.

If you are launching a product, keep all of the marketing materials you used and a timeline of what you did.

Shy Bairns Get Nowt

It's an old saying from where I come from (translation – shy children get nothing). What it means is that if you don't ask then you don't get. If there is something that you want to do in your business or a joint venture partner you want to work with or some publicity that you want then you need to go ask for it. If you don't ask then you don't get. What's the worst that can happen? They say no? Well as least then you know rather than guessing.

Distraction is the devil

Distraction is bad for business. Don't let yourself fall into massively distracting activities on a day to day basis – for example, where you spend your time flicking through your social media newsfeed, looking for something, anything, staring like you are looking for an answer. It's a time drain and you mustn't convince yourself that that is working. You can lose hours of time to the social media vortex and it's not cool. You can turn around and suddenly you have lost 2 hours. Okay you might have seen a cute piccie of Nicola's dog and seen some funny MEMEs and Sarah's kids' school photos but you haven't done anything productive. If you can't control yourself there are apps available that will prohibit you from certain websites for certain periods of time.

Where's the wastage?

Make sure you don't have a drain in your business. It's often the case that we purchase subscriptions that we never use and that we buy things before thinking them through properly. Now's the time to do an audit on your expenditure. What are you paying too much for? Which subscriptions can you cancel? What else do you need to do in order to plug the money drains?

Be seen or be no-one

I can't say this too many times. You HAVE TO STOP HIDING. If you are not being seen then no-one will know that you exist. If no-one knows you exist then no one can buy from you. You must do all you can to be seen. You need to court the attention of your fans on social media, you need to put yourself forwards for PR and Guest Blogs, you need to be prepared to have a marketing budget to gain exposure.

Don't Grow A Beast

Find your happy place. Find your happy place to work, a happy place to interact with your crowd and a happy place within your business. DO NOT GROW A BEAST. If you don't love your business right now then don't seek to grow it – you will simply grow a beast. This is one thing I have seen in reality so many times.

I gotta admit that I have never got to the point of hating my business but there have been times when it's been significantly out of whack.

I remember one occasion vividly, it was at a VIP day I was hosting and the first thing that I asked the room was "do you love your business right now?". I got some all in (truly, madly, deeply) kinda head nods, I got some "hhhhmmmmm well, I'm not sure" responses and I got tears. Tears to the realisation that they didn't love their business right now, in that moment.

The realisation is painful because that's when the light strikes with a white hot flame of truth that you have in fact self-styled and grown a beast. A beast that does not serve you, a beast that feels out of whack, a beast that has more control than you do and what do you do? You keep blindly running with the beast thinking that it will get better and that things will get easier but the reality is that you don't change anything and you continue to feed the beast and the beast continues to grow. STOP!

The first thing you need to do is recognise it. Ask yourself the question, muse over it, take the question to a coffee shop or out for a walk – Do You Love Your Business Right Now? If the answer is anything but a hell yeah! then you need to STOP and take stock.

Now, loving a business is kinda like loving a child, there'll be some behaviours that aren't your shit hot favourites and there'll be some activities that you do for the sake of your child that don't actually light you up (my kids don't make me do their accounts but you get the gist). That doesn't mean that as you cosy up at the end of the day you don't love them truly, madly, deeply. So in business you will sometimes have to do shit you don't wanna do but you'll do it because it's good for your business. You'll learn to play to your strengths and you'll learn how to avoid tantrums and things being out of whack. Some days it'll frustrate you and piss you off but it will be your all and everything and you'll love it fiercely.

Ok, so if we've answered "no" then here are some questions you need to consider:

- Recognition – recognise that you are feeling a little lost. We can often try to push down the feel and we can look to box it off and ignore it. We are pushing at the coal face and we can be inclined to keep on keeping on. But recognising that we feel a little lost means that we can start to see what we can do about it.
- Don't Grow A Monster – if you're not happy with your business or your life or anything in between then please don't keep growing it. The last thing you want to do is grow a big old beast that doesn't serve you. If it's not

right now then a bigger version of that will serve you even less.

- Acceptance – accept that it might be that you need to make changes, it might be small tweaks but it might be a change in direction and know that this is totally ok.
- Step Away – when you are so close to everything that you can't see the big picture. Step away a little, do something fun, do something that makes you smile and give yourself a break. Often when we are focusing so intently on something we simply can't see the way forward, but when we step away we allow the direction to simply find us. Ideas will flow, solutions will become more obvious and you will gain clarity in the situation.
- Discharge It of Its Power – so often our personal reactions and emotions to what is going on gives the situation much more power than it deserves. Try to look at things objectively or speak to someone else about it who may offer you a totally different and valuable viewpoint.
- Realign With Your Mission – what is it that you are actually here to do? What is the mission? Who are you here to serve? What do you want to change in the world? What do you want to change in your world? Why do you do what you do? (<< Write those questions down and answer them – allow your passion to flow back into your work.)
- If in Doubt Serve the Pants Off Your Fans – step into a place of giving, step back into service. Immerse yourself in helping your fans and your audience. When you step back into purely serving your fans then the other stuff will look after itself. You will gain more clarity about what it is you do and how you can bring more forth and get back on track.

Whatever you do, stop blindly growing the beast!

It's all in the image

Don't underestimate the power of images. Imagery works in your social media to stop the scroll, in your blogs to break up text or illustrate a point, your sales pages to make them feel more visual. Imagery is massively important in your marketing for so many reasons and getting a brand "look and feel" to your imagery will mean that people recognise your imagery quickly, and that your brand has much more about it.

Pictures and visuals are so important in your business. Not only do they say that a picture paints a thousand words BUT it's more than that for Rockstars.

It's important that you have professional images of yourself to use on your website and Social Media (your holiday piccies aren't going to cut it).

It's also important that you think through the images that you will use in your marketing.

- Do they tie in with your branding?
- Will they be eye- catching within people's newsfeeds?
- Will they catch attention and stop people scrolling?
- If you are adding text to the image can it be read with ease?
- Does it look professional or like it has just been shoved together?

Remember, everything that you put "out there" is an ambassador for your brand – and that reflection can either be positive, negative or "meh" There are two of those reflections that you NEED to avoid.

Self Invest

Invest in yourself – you are the driving force in your business. Your energy moves your business forward and you need to make sure you are investing in yourself – it might be through self-care, fitness, eating well, or learning new things; whatever it is make sure you are filling your cup and looking after yourself.

Pop It On A Post It

Post-it notes are for more than scribbling down a quick reminder. They are great for planning. I use them to plan programmes, social media posts, my books and more. The great thing about post-it notes is that you can shift them around and have a visual on what you're planning before committing it to a mind map or plan.

Ascension?

Remember to consider a "client ascension path" – JEEZ that sounds dull & official, doesn't it?!! I like to look at it as a "what's next?" kinda approach. If people come to your social media platform – what's next? If people read that blog – what's next? If people sign up for that freebie – what's next? If people buy that product – what's next?

Business Isn't Eyeliner

Strategy is key – big businesses don't wing it.

So here's the thing. There's a happy blend between being organised and having a plan, and being able to work within your flow.

Don't get me wrong - I do love a plan and I am totes in love with planning sessions BUT I am also careful not to over-plan, and the rebel in me says that it's ok to do your planning as and when it feels right for you and when you have the space & peace to do it. I suppose it's all about the fact that planning is for life and not just for Christmas.

If you don't want to use any planning tools, then that's totally cool. If you do, then that's perfect too. It's all about what works for you.

I love handwriting plans and goals and targets - for me there's power in the written word BUT you might prefer to grab an app or open a Trello board or type them up or create a dream board - again, do what works for you.

I have time taken out of my diary quarterly to catch up on directional planning and strategy because I don't like to micro plan too far in advance because that produces rigidity and keeps me stuck.

Planning is what you want it to be.

Planning can take place whenever you want it to.

Don't panic, you aren't inferior if you haven't planned out the next year and it's not a sign that you haven't got your shit together. It merely is what it is.

Don't let the thought of planning or your plans overwhelm you.

235

Everything is massive until you break it down and look at the individual steps you need to take. Planning a year is HUGE – 365 days of doing and whilst an overarching view from above will serve you massively it's ok if you haven't got to what that view looks like just yet.

You aren't BEHIND!

It's all totally ok.

Wherever you are and however much planning you have already done (or not) isn't a reflection on your ability or your future, it won't make you a success or a failure. Taking action, being present, having direction and a good mindset is what will make all the difference – the plans will just help you nail the other stuff.

Whether it's done, whether you do it tomorrow, this month or later in the year it's your call.

Remember, that your most important resource in your business is your time, planning and strategy are important but should definitely NOT become a time drain.

- Don't waste time on a planner if you are never going to use it.
- You don't need to plan what to put in your planner.
- Don't buy every planner on the market like you are seeking some magic solution to something.
- Plans don't work unless you do.
- Planners that never see the light of day after you have spent hours and hours crafting them will not bring you

an additional income.
- Planners that never get written in are a waste of money.
- Don't waste days on your planner if you need to be doing other things.
- My advice to you is that planning and strategy in your business is for life and not just for Christmas.
- Don't buy multiple planners.
- Don't hold on to the dream that one planning session will bring you all the answers.
- You don't have to buy a planner – you can plan in a Word document, on your phone, in an app or in a (very beautiful) notebook.
- Plan + Execution = the difference.
- Plan on BUT do it mindfully.

Don't be flaky

Flaky is so easy to fall into. You decide that you are going to do something, then for whatever reason, you spit your dummy and it's no longer part of the masterplan OR you set out on a big launch and don't get the reaction you want immediately and then give up. Flaky won't help you grow. There are times when, once you have committed to doing something, you must keep pushing forwards. Not only will you most likely see results come if you continue (you'll definitely get no results if you give up) but you'll also learn stacks along the way.

No substance = no service

Make sure that your marketing and your website and your message have substance. If you have no substance then you are of no service to your fans. One of the prime examples of this is the whole "peacocking" thing that lots of coaches seem to be doing in their live webinars. They get people to sign-up to their calls on the promise of some fantastic content. They make a big promise. Often one that is far from truthful like, "Listen to this webinar and I will show you how to make a zillion pounds on your first launch". Anyhaps, that aside, what results is a webinar where they spend the majority of the time talking about themselves and then a sales pitch, somewhere sandwiched in the middle is a tiny bit of substance. That's not what people sign up for and it's not my idea of providing value to your crowd. My live calls include REAL LIFE substance. Regardless of whether you buy from me or not (if it's a sales call) you will be able to take something away from the call and implement it into your business. I think that substance and content MUST be central to your service.

Quotes are cool but aren't going to give you a Rockstar brand

Don't rely on guff and fluff to build your business. Motivational and inspirational quotes most likely have a place in your business but it's important that you don't become a business without any substance. Guff & fluff will attract followers but not necessarily the right people, not necessarily people who will turn into customers. A Rockstar will have a fantastic marketing mix which includes quotes and inspiration but the motivation is often more than just quotes from others and you can provide much more inspiration to your fans than a quote from someone they have never heard of. Make sure you substance.

I HAVE NO TIME!!

That is merely the story you are telling yourself. We all have the same amount of time in a day, we all have the same number of days in a week. We all have busy lives and things outside of our business to do. We all get caught up in stuff that we shouldn't be doing. Your time management is important. You need to get help with the stuff that's sucking time away from you. It might be that you need to avoid the supermarket and start doing your shopping online, it might be that you need a cleaner, it might be that you need to outsource some of your admin and bookkeeping. If you go into a poverty mindset (regardless of whether that's financial poverty or time poverty) then all you seem to do is exaggerate that situation. You become more time poor because you spend time worrying about being time poor – ironic I know!!

Your most precious business asset is your time – don't waste it, don't give it away to those who don't respect it, and don't muck about with it. You can't make more time, you can't get the time back that you have used.

Can I find you?

If I was looking for someone like you, but didn't know you, would I be able to find you? I know that that sounds massively confusing. If I was struggling with the things that your fans struggle with then how would I find you? What words am I likely to pop into the search engine, what copy am I likely to resonate with? If I popped those things into Google then will you come up? Google yourself and see what happens! Then Google what your fans might be Googling (without using your name or your business name) and see what happens then!

Talk it through – you've forgotten how much you know – the big bad CURSE OF KNOWLEDGE.

We all suffer from this one. We all forget exactly how much we know and what it's like not to know that. Your Mastermind specialist subject is what you teach to your crowd. You need to remember that just because it comes naturally to you, other people don't have this knowledge or skill with ease like you do. What would it feel like not to know the things you teach? What do you need to do to take it back to basics? Which parts of your business have gaps (all because you have forgotten how much you know and the fact that your crowd may be absolute beginners)? I often suggest that you talk through your specialist subject with someone. Someone who isn't an expert as they will ask you questions and tease your full knowledge out of you.

The Raving Fans Notebook

One of my favourites and one that I suggest every business owner has. My lovely clients are all encouraged to have one and make the most of it. So, what is it? It's a single place where you put all your information about your fans. It has multiple purposes. It allows you to collect lots of information about your fans which will inspire your copy writing but it will also merge with your specialist subject to become your place of inspiration, your place to re-connect with your audience at times when you feel disconnected. You can dive in there and pull out blog ideas, ideas for programmes, take in your fans psyche before you write your sales page.

Grab the resources on how to create yours >> www. beabusinessrockstar.com_

How much is enough?

Usually more than is comfortable. I am a firm believer in over delivering. When you first start out you will need to give away for free much more than is comfy. You need to include more in your programme than you think (but that doesn't mean that you add everything that you know – often it's more of the basics). Always seek to give more to your crowd than they expect. What you must be careful of is that you don't blow all of your ideas in one blog or one programme or one call >> what you'll do there is that you will overwhelm your fans, you will paralyse them into inaction and it'll mean that your content will become harder for you in the long run.

Do You Need To Leverage

A leveraged income ISN'T for everyone but do consider if you only sell time for money (1-2-1/done for you work) then you will run out of time to sell, you will get to a point where you are resistant to putting up your prices anymore and you will ultimately burn out. You can't magic up more time.

Team Up

Consider collaborations. You can get together with other entrepreneurs in official collaborative/joint venture arrangements or you can simply agree to share each other's stuff.

You need to be looking for someone who is speaking to a similar audience to you but who isn't offering the same products/ services. How can you work together in order to cross- pollinate each other's businesses?

Why pricing makes you pale

Pricing will make you address every issue that you have ever had go through your head about self-worth. You will judge yourself against others and pop ycurself into a hierarchy. You will doubt yourself, you will undervalue yourself and you will talk yourself out of charging what you're worth (because you will doubt how much you are worth).

Don't be frightened of pricing.

Firstly – stop thinking that you are psychic and know what people are able, willing or prepared to pay. Even if you are psychic it's not your psychic prowess talking here, this is your ego and this is self-talk at work!

Secondly – look at the value! Whct will your clients be able to be/do/have if they take you up on your offer?

Thirdly – this is about fair exchange! Your clients need to be in fair exchange with you for your awesomeness.

Enough of the self-talk, align to the price, practice saying it out loud and steer clear of the negative self-talk (as soon as the negative self-talk takes hold you will be waving your clients forth with one hand and pushing them away with the other). << We don't want that!

#Rude

People can be unintentionally rude.

I am SUPER tolerant, laid back & easy going most of the time.

I will go that extra mile and am driven to help. It's the way I am. I care and I care an awful lot.

What does get my goat is the fact that I encounter (not regularly) people who seem to have left their manners at home. I don't need you to thank me and thank me for stuff that I do, I am not wanting any recognition or a pat on the back. I'm simply suggesting that people remember to say please & thank you and don't spend demanding emails and messages. I know that we work in a very instantaneous society and I know that most people certainly don't mean for their communications to sound this way BUT it happens.

I do type messages in haste when I'm busy but I always go back and make sure that I have added in all the niceties within the communication before I hit send.

I self-edit too.

Sometimes my buttons get pushed and I want to make a little issue of it BUT it's not necessary, it's not worth my energy. I have to reassure myself that the likelihood is that they didn't mean to demand and come across a little rude.

Anyhaps, moral of the story, in the same way as "think before you speak" make sure you have a little scan read before you press send.

Belly Fires

Do whatever lights a fire in your belly. "If it is still in your mind, it's worth the risk." Paulo Coelho.

Focus Focus Focus

You won't get the results you want if you aren't focusing on the right things.

If your focus is purely money and numbers = you won't get the results you want. If you don't continue to focus on service = you won't get the results you want.

If you think no-one will buy = you won't get the results you want.

If you don't offer people the opportunity and try to hide sales messages = you won't get the results you want.

Thinking the right things and taking the right action = getting the results you want!!

You won't get the results you want if you give up. I know that during launch periods people can get tired, they can get disheartened, they can get sick of talking about their products/ services – but it's important to see it through, keep going, realign with the love of your product and service and tell people about it. If you give up you'll never know what you could have achieved if you'd seen it through.

Don't Undervalue Yourself

Don't undervalue yourself. Your time is precious, you are an expert and you don't need to be "cheap".

Don't be a garage door when it comes to selling.

If all the garage doors are the same then there's no way to have a favourite - if there are no differences other than price then all you ever do if base your purchase on price.

If all the garage doors are exactly the same then you'll buy the cheapest garage door. Make sure you are differentiating what you do by more than a price tag! #justsaying

Selling Sucks?

Selling doesn't have to be icky. You can do it in an absolutely heart-centred way. Think about how you can show your crowd the problems they can solve or the issues that they can overcome by buying from you. I don't wanna use the word "pitch" but I suppose it's the word that sums it up the best. A synopsis that encourages them to purchase. Think about what's in it for them and how you solve their problems. Xx

Integrity

Integrity is EVERYTHING #enoughsaid.

EVERYONE NEEDS HELP!

Biz owners need to get out of their own way and gain an outsider view and perspective. They need assistance from someone who isn't too close and that can see the overall picture. You can't run your business like a toddler "I do it all by myself." It's ok to draft in some help from the outside, not because they are failing but because they want to succeed.

Notebook Control

Carry a notebook or record ideas on your phone on the go – don't let them run away from you.

Where are you keeping all of your notes?

I know that it's really easy to have a gazillon notebooks and systems on the go all at once and that you can end up wasting hours and hours looking for ideas that you have had and things that you want to implement.

How do I break this down?

I have 1 notebook (which I fill before starting a new one) for my business.

I have 1 notebook for client calls and the notes from their calls.

I have Trello boards for stuff that is settled and will continue to be used (so once implemented and action has been taken the notes can be safely stored there – for example my launch process for a product, my testimonials, my longer Facebook posts etc, each has a board and they are stored for recycling and re-using).

My phone – when I'm out and about I make notes of ideas on my phone and take lots of pictures. I then process them periodically into action steps and they either go into the notebook for further thought or they are actioned at that time.

Don't make it too hard, don't have too many places to find your notes.

Simple but significant is the mantra as always.

Whatever you do - don't have stacks of bits of paper and never be able to find anything

Bad days are normal – just keep perspective

I'm sorry to tell you that you will never be content, as soon as you reach one goal the next one will be added to the list. As soon as you master one thing a new thing will present itself for you to learn. The most important skill you will learn is how to get out of your own way, how to recognise when you need time off and how to keep your momentum going when you're having a bad day. I have written a blog recently about bad days. My hubby came home from a double fatality of two youngish boys the other week. I'm not telling you this to make you feel guilty but some people's bad days are much worse than ours. What we need to do is to plan for the bad days, take time off, have pick-me-ups. It's easy to do what I used to do and work yourself into the ground. You can't see the wood for the trees, you can't make decent decisions in your business because your view is blurry (this is why I dare you to schedule some time off). You need to be kind to yourself, you need to appreciate how far you have come and you need to remember all those people you help. You are an expert in your field and you are bloomin awesome.

Turn The Pressure Cooker Off

Stop putting so much pressure on yourself!

Chances are, if you release the immense pressure, magical things will happen!

I spoke to a lady a little while ago who used the word "pressure" when we talked about her work. We decided that the word needed reframing. She needed to look at things a different way.

The pressure of too much work – it's a lesson about how much you should take on at one time, a lesson in the management of your own personal expectations of yourself (and perhaps client expectations too) and an opportunity to serve lots of people.

The pressure of not having enough work (and I'm not being flippant here – I've been there and I know it's a big deal) is a lesson in patience at times (Rome wasn't built in a day). It's a lesson in making things happen and a compelling cry to take positive action and it's a lesson in the fact that when you look for it there's opportunity in all sorts of places.

Pressure is the exact feeling of that pressure cooker; it's consuming, it's overwhelming, it
feels like you might just explode. You can't do your best work when you feel this way.

Step back.

Give yourself some time off. Helicopter out and take a full view of potential and possibility.

Keep your eyes open for opportunity.

Release the pressure and step back into the flow.

Pre-empt It Petal

Answer your clients' concerns before they have even asked

248

them. Think about the concerns and objections your client may have and make sure you give an honest and open response within your marketing, on sales pages or on a frequently asked questions page.

What can I Do Today?

Ask yourself each morning – what can I do to serve the pants off my crowd? what do I want to achieve today? What's on my urgent action list? What would I love to get done (but isn't critical) and what can I do to serve the pants off my crowd today?

Not Everyone Will Support You

Not everyone will support you – I know it's sad to even type it. ☹

There will be people who support you or are inspired by you – there are others who, for whatever reason (and it's their stuff and not yours) will not be supportive and will take swipes and bites at you.

Always remember that it's a reflection of them and not you!

What's The Diagnosis

It's easy to diagnose things as a bit broken.

I see lots of people who feel angsty about the development of their business.
I know you are impatient and I know that sometimes things in life don't feel like they are moving in the right direction.

Whether you feel like you are wading through treacle, or it feels like you are shouting down deep dark holes, or the enormity feels overwhelming, or you question constantly whether you are actually cut out for this shit, I want you to know it's normal.

We all have days where it feels a little hard.

Lots of us ain't great with the whole patience thing.

We want progress but we get stuck.

What I want you to do is be careful how you diagnose things. The language we use and the diagnosis we attach to when things feel a little shit can keep us stuck.

When you declare you're "stuck" all the time or "wading through treacle" or "overwhelmed" you are programming the energetic charge of these words into your world.

Step back.

Write down where you are right now. There's power in that there pen and the act of writing it out immediately discharges the emotion for the situation and allows you to see it in its bare reality.

Look for solutions and don't get lost in problems.

Take action and don't just think about it.

You can't hand your life over to the Universe and expect to be brought the best version of yourself, or your success, or the business of your dreams.

This is a combination of thinking the right way and doing the right things.

It's about sidestepping the stuck.

It's about being careful of the language you use and the diagnosis you bequeath on the situation.

Smile more.

Search for solutions.

Stop getting stuck.

Mind your language and don't encourage the energetic charge of negativity to be running through your days.

It's ok to get stuck, to feel overwhelmed and to get angsty. WHAT'S NOT OK is to stay there and attach an ongoing diagnosis.

Everyone Isn't Your Client

Don't be afraid to turn work away. Listen to your gut, if it's screaming NO then take notice as those are usually the ones that cause more angst or energy than they are worth.

Remember the impact you have

Just you remember how your expertise changes lives. As I edit this book I have had a meeting with a VIP client. She said to me that you forget the kind of impact you make. She makes a massive impact into the world of others and helps them in circumstances when they are at their lowest ebb. She often doesn't know that she's doing it at the time, that is until she gets messages and emails of thanks. But what do you do? What impact do you make? This lovely lady said to me that I forget the impact that I make, yes I help people grow their business but for her that has meant that she can look after her family, buy her dream house, pick her little lady up from school as well as help hundreds of souls around the world. Now that's a true blessing.

Avoid Burnout

Burnout sucks.

I want you to know that I totally ge⁻ it and it's ok not to be ok.

So, right now, your head feels like a heady mix of cotton wool, mashed potato with perhaps a side order of clouds. Everything you try to do feels like you are wading through treacle. Why is it all so hard?

Your creativity isn't firing on all cylinders.

Your mojo took a hike.

Your enthusiasm is waning.

Your body aches.

Regardless of how much sleep you are getting you feel totally and utterly exhausted.

You don't wanna stop, you wanna continue pushing because surely if you stop you are going to drop the ball, you won't be serving your clients and everything is going to go tits up.

So you keep wading. AND things don't get any better. Surely, there must be something wrong with you. You have this overwhelming exhaustion. This can't be normal.

Now, I'm not a doctor and if you think that you have something amiss then it's VITAL that you get that shit checked out. You owe it to yourself to take care of you because without you there's no business.

NOW, let's talk about burn out.

Ignore these signs for too long and you will be forced to stop, you will be forced to step back and you will really have no choice. I've seen people push through, I've seen people trying to do stuff that they are simply not feeling, and pushing harder and harder. Now's the perfect time to tell you that all which is pushed moves away from you, all which is chased makes a run in the opposite direction.

So, let's just stop a moment.

We don't want this to turn into out and out burnout. We know that bad boy has its own rules and it may stop you for a week, a month, a quarter or even longer. I've seen the fallout of this. I've seen amazing people side-lined. Worn out. Burnt out.

I'm not going to beat about the bush with this one nor am I going to offer you a magic way to avoid this. The first thing you need to do is get much more self-aware.

Pushing and pushing means things move away from you. It's not going to develop your business, it's going to make everything trickier. I get that you have to put the work in and particularly in the first stages of building your business you have to do everything yourself. Your business has effectively become your baby and needs your care and attention – even when you're not with it, you are thinking about it and the guilt of leaving it without your attention can be massively overwhelming.

I know that in the early stages of business I certainly rode the wave of burnout on occasions. There were times where I was in my office, after the kids were in bed, deep into the wee hours.

Then the more you do it the more you want to keep doing it, you feel then the obligation to continue to put ridiculous hours in, and you turn into a mean boss.

So managing your energy means that you have to look after yourself – if self-care makes you slow blink, roll your eyes or even poke them out then you might wanna consider the fact that if you had a machine in your business and didn't take care of it then it would eventually break, and then you wouldn't get any work done, you'd lose money and it'd take time to sort the problem out. YOU ARE THAT MACHINE - EXCEPT YOU ARE NOT REPLACEABLE!! If you need to think about self-care a little differently.

So if you are on the cusp of burnout right now, what should you do?

STOP – it's super fab that you have recognised it but you need to just stop for a moment, settle (even if it's just for a moment) and inhale! The constant-ness of your action has been exhausting and overwhelming. Chances are that you haven't taken a great big deep inhale for AGES!

REFLECT – take a look at what you are doing right now – are you busy or are you productive? Busy and productive aren't the same thing. Do a little list of where you are spending your time. Are you wasting lots of time on social media? Are you spending time in (dis)organised chaos? Are you doing jobs that you actually don't need to do anymore and are merely completing out of habit?

DITCH, DELEGATE, DO – which of the jobs can you ditch? Which can you get some help and support with? Which do YOU need to do?

CLEAR THE DECKS – work through and get rid of the stuff that's pissing you off – that will then open up some bandwidth for you and allow you a little more space.

I HAVE A LITTLE CHALLENGE – if I am ever tempted to fall into overworking (and at times it's tempting because I bloody love what I do) I implement a little 7-7 challenge. I shut down at 7pm and don't do anything work related until after 7am and wherever possible I stay off line during those periods too – this gives me a little downtime.

FOCUS – start to focus more on the task in hand rather than masses of multi-tasking, and make sure you aren't falling into the social media vortex and spending time that you are dressing up as work flicking through your social media timeline.

FILL YOUR CUP – do stuff that fills your cup, revitalises you and gives you more energy – whatever that means for you!

GET REAL – stop taking on too much work that you are battling all of the time, prioritise your diary, make time to work on stuff that needs your attention.

CHECK OUT ENERGY DRAINS – do you have any particular clients or projects that are taking up too much of your time and energy and you aren't in fair exchange on those projects? You may need to re-look at the relationship, the boundaries or end that working relationship with that particular client.

IMPLEMENT GOOD BOUNDARIES – and self-boundaries might be the biggest one you need to look at here. I know you absolutely want to help your clients but you mustn't do that at the cost of your own health and well-being.

I want you to know that you aren't a #fail for ending up feeling this way – it's about making sure that burnout waves don't keep consuming you and ultimately wash you away because that leaves the decisions out of your hands.

13 WHERE YOU NEED TO GO PRO

Photos – have professional photos taken for your business. You need a photographer to get some perfect pictures that match your brand for you to use on your website and social media. Cropping down your holiday piccies just won't cut it. Get those photos updated regularly. I don't care what lies you are telling yourself about getting your pro photos done when you have lost 20lbs etc. Your fans love you – just as you are!

Email Management System – you MUST NOT try to do this one on the cheap. You CANNOT send out your emails to your list from your regular email account. You must use an email management system to ensure that you are complying with data protection legislation and spamming laws. Your fans need to have an opportunity to unsubscribe from your emails (and that's not a bad thing – those who unsubscribe just weren't that into you anyway and weren't going to buy from you).

Course Delivery – when you are delivering your online courses it's important that you go pro. When you try to deliver your programmes via email, not only do they look amateur-ish but you end up making more work for yourself. People delete emails, you end up in SPAM bins and you aren't making it easy for your fans to consume what they have bought from you.

Your Assets – stop trying to work on a computer that's falling apart. I did it for a long while. I was frightened of making additional investments in my business and I had convinced myself that everything was working ok. But what was actually happening was that I was wasting time – time I could have been spending on income generating activities.

Invest in Yourself – when you stop growing, you stop growing. You need to invest in your business and moving your business forwards. You can't skip this step. You need to continue to learn and develop your skill set, your business savvy skills and your marketing.

Your Website – this is your shop window to the world. You need to make sure that that shop window is the best that it can be.

Your Team – you don't need to do this all by yourself and it's best that you don't do it all by yourself. Gather a dream team around you to help you fly higher and faster than you could ever do alone.

AND FINALLY....

I know you have a fire in your belly! – I am not going to shout and swear at you. I'm not going to get you to the point whereby you believe you have to prove me wrong. I will never put you down or make you feel pants. I will not tell you that it's my way or the high way. I ain't that type of girl. I know you have a fire in your belly. I know that you want to make this work. I know that

that burning desire is there. Sometimes that fire in your belly dulls a little and other times it's shining bright all by itself. I know that you often have a burning desire to prove yourself or other people wrong BUT I know that most of all you want to make this business a success. That you want to make everything work. I know you can do it and that you just need to harness that fire in your belly – you can do this!

You can't be a Rockstar without a plan. It's now time to set yourself up for success. It's pointless running a business without a plan. You're never going to reach your full potential whilst winging it.

So here's how the journey begins...

- Roll up your socks and decide that you are going to do this.
- Commit to yourself and your sanity that you will get out of your own way, you will stop overthinking stuff.
- Commit to going pro. Stop cutting corners and doing things on the cheap.
- Stand out and make sure that you aren't just blending into the scenery and being vanilla.
- Do stuff often that scares the pants off you. Pack your comfort blanket in your handbag and leave behind the comfort zone. Keep going and keep growing.
- Be yourself – loud & proud >> no filter.
- Take your time and make good decisions.
- Serve your fans & respect their time, money & attention.
- Be brave.
- Remember, nothing changes if you change nothing!

- Remember that you need to take action to make changes.
- You need to be bold.
- You need to put yourself out there and move through the fear. Fear is natural, it's a sign of growth, greet it as a friend and not an enemy.
- Progress loves action.
- Commit today to taking action on your dreams (even on days when you don't feel like it)!

66

"Do or Do Not. There Is Not Try."
Yoda

MORE STUFF & BONUSES

Beyond Ordinary – the book that looks at what it takes to elevate your business beyond the status of ordinary. We are focusing a lot around mindset, creativity and getting out of your own way in a big way in this book!

Social Media With Soul – your guide to not shouting down deep dark holes on social media, particularly on Facebook. We are talking showing up, engagement and interacting with your audience.

Bonus Links

Don't forget to grab your goodies and the FREE MP3 version of the book that you can download and listen to on the go. All your bonus links can be accessed here:

www.beabusinessrockstar.com

Here's a reminder of what's waiting for you...

- How to put together an amazing crowd notebook
- RavingFans' Workbook
- Video – How to share things from other people's pages that you think will resonate with your fans – doing it ethically
- Freebies That Fly Ebook
- Numbers tracker

Come say "Hi"

Facebook: EmmaHolmesRebelsandRockstars

Twitter: @rebelsandrockstars

LinkedIn: emmaholmes5

Instagram: @rebelsandrockstars

Resources Link: www.imaflippingrockstar.com

Want more: www.rebelsandrockstars.com

About Emma

Emma Holmes is the Proud Owner and Founder of Rebels & Rockstars: a hatchery for entrepreneurs with soul.

Helping heart-centred and soulful entrepreneurs to build ridiculously big businesses is her vocation, and she still pinches herself sometimes, that this is actually her job. (She used to be a lawyer who loved living in corporate land, but when mummy guilt arrived, she challenged herself to a new adventure.)

Emma's also an outsource cheerleader, and a spiritual but practical kind of soul. And she is definitely not scared of a challenge. (She set herself the biggest challenge of her self-employed life in 2015 – to grow a £100k online business without using the 'tried-and-tested icky sales techniques' that £100k biz owners usually resorted to.)

Her 2015 success story has since been put to good use (many times), and Emma is positively thrilled to have helped her clients with some pretty amazing online launches - 18k income in one day, launches of £54k+ in sales, and a 30K in 30 days project are just a tiny snapshot of her clients' achievements.

But what makes Emma beyond ordinary is that she has her own interpretation of business success, and it isn't about totting up your bank balance. She knows real, long-lasting business success is about creating a sustainable business you love, which grows naturally, fits around your lifestyle and family, and enables your authenticity, and sparkly personality to shine.

As well as being a real-life human blogging machine, Emma has also been featured on That's Manchester TV and BBC Radio. She's written for Business Rocks, Freelance Parenting, Fresh Business Thinking, Talented Ladies Club, and MeMeMe.

In a nutshell, she's proud to be a square peg who doesn't care about round holes and fitting in boxes. And she encourages her clients to do the same.

Lightning Source UK Ltd.
Milton Keynes UK
UKHW05f0023210818
327522UK00009B/193/P

9 781999 722869